PHP Interview Questions, Answers, and Explanations: PHP Certification Review

Compiled By Terry Sanchez

PHP Interview Questions, Answers, and Explanations:
PHP Certification Review

ISBN 10 : 1-933804-41-6
ISBN 13: 978-1-933804-41-5

Edited By: Jamie Fisher

Printed in the United States of America

Please visit our website at www.itcookbook.com

Table of Contents

Question 01: PHP array values with Javascript

Questions have come up in the Javascript forum a number of times recently regarding dynamically generated form fields where that names contain the [] characters like:

```
<input type="text" name="myField[]">
```

They want to be able to address the fields via Javascript but it has trouble with the [] in the field names.

Is there a workaround so that these names could be rendered Javascript friendly without impairing the function on the PHP side?

A: Use the attribute "id".

If you have a form field formatted as:

```
<input type="text" name="thefield[0]"
id="thefield_0"...>
```

You can use the id value in your object references in JavaScript:

```
document. ... .thefield_0.value
```

Question 02: Print Array - Columned HTML

I want to print an array which contains about 50 elements into an HTML table with 4 columns. I want to display four keys (records) by row instead of one key by row.

It's something like this:

CODE:

```
+----------+----------+----------+----------+
|Key1      |Key2      |Key3      |Key4      |
+----------+----------+----------+----------+
|Key5      |Key6      |Key7      |Key8      |
+----------+----------+----------+----------+
```

Obviously with my current code, I simply print everything on the same row. I guess I would have to loop a string to define the record number and etc...

CODE:

```
<table cellpadding="0" cellspacing="0" border"0">
    <tr>
foreach ($Pages as $key=>$Page) {
    print "<td>$Page['Title']</td>";
}
    </tr>
</table>


[code]
$Pages = array(

    "50" => array (
            "Title" => "some text 50",
            "Desc" => "some text",
            "Content" => "some text" ),
    "51" => array (
            "Title" => "some text 51",
```

```
                    "Desc" => "some text",
                    "Content" => "some text" ),
      "52" => array (
                    "Title" => "some text 52",
                    "Desc" => "some text",
                    "Content" => "some text" ),
      "53" => array (
                    "Title" => "some text 53",
                    "Desc" => "some text",
                    "Content" => "some text"),
```

What can I do make this work?

A: You need an additional check on whether the array has finished at an uneven point so that you can properly terminate the row. Use this code instead:

CODE:
```
<table cellpadding="0" cellspacing="0" border"0">
<?
$cnt = 1;
$tot_c = 0;
$tot = count($Pages);
foreach ($Pages as $key=>$Page):
$tot_c++;
switch ($cnt):
case 1:
echo "<tr><td>{$Page['Title']}</td>";
$cnt++;
break;
case 4:
echo "<td>{$Page['Title']}</td></tr>";
$cnt = 1;
break;
case 2:
echo "<td>{$Page['Title']}</td>";
if ($tot_c === $tot) echo
"<td> </td><td> </td></tr>";
break;
case 3:
echo "<td>{$Page['Title']}</td>";
if ($tot_c === $tot) echo "<td> </td></tr>";
$cnt++;
break;
endswitch;
endforeach;
```

```
?>
</table>
```

I'd recommend using CSS though, its cleaner:

CODE:
```
<?
<style tye="text/css">
.cell {width:10em; padding:1px;}
.cells {width: 44em;}
</style>
echo "<div class=\"cells\">";
foreach ($Pages as $key=>$Page):
echo "<span class=\"cell\">{$Page['Title']}</span>";
endforeach;
echo "</div>";
```

Question 03: Multidimensional Array - Print Key

I have the following m-dim array and I would like to know how to print the "Key" (50,51,52,53...).

CODE:
```
$Pages = array(
    "50" => array (
                "Title" => "some text 50",
                "Desc" => "some text",
                "Content" => "some text" ),
    "51" => array (
                "Title" => "some text 51",
                "Desc" => "some text",
                "Content" => "some text" ),
    "52" => array (
                "Title" => "some text 52",
                "Desc" => "some text",
                "Content" => "some text" ),
    "53" => array (
                "Title" => "some text 53",
                "Desc" => "some text",
                "Content" => "some text" ),
);
```

CODE:
```
foreach ($Pages as $P) {
    print $P['Title'] . $P . "<br>";
}
```

What is the correct code to print the "keys"?

A: This code should work for you:

CODE:
```
foreach ($Pages as $key=>$page):
    echo "Array key $key has title element
{$page['Title']} <br/>";
endforeach;
```

Question 04: Variable names into variable values

I am developing a rental website for multiple properties and need an availability calendar for it. The client side of the calendar is fine and works (it takes booking details for certain days out of a mysql database). I am having problems in creating the admin side of it where renters can update their properties' availability. At the moment for testing purposes, I have entered details into the mysql manually using phpmyadmin.

What I want is a full year or month to be displayed and for the owner to be able to tick radio boxes for each day, submit the data (by month or a year) and for that data to be written to the database.

I need to dynamically create the option name so it is something like 20060503 - i.e. today's date YYYY/MM/DD.

How can I make the script to automatically parse the form, getting the option name and then inserting either U or B (unavailable or booked) into the database which is set up as a mysql date field (which would be the option name) and an option field which is an enum of U or B?

A: I strongly recommend that you not use dynamic variable names.

There is an obscure feature of PHP that if form field names are formatted the right way, PHP will treat the values of those forms as arrays. For example, if you have the form:

```
<form method="post" action="somescript.php">
    <input type="text" name="foo[1]"><br>
    <input type="text" name="foo[2]"><br>
    <input type="text" name="foo[3]"><br>
    <input type="submit">
</form>
```

Then when submitted, $_POST['foo'] will itself be an array of three elements, each element containing one of the input values.

To apply this to your question, if I have the HTML;

```
<html><body>
<form method="post" action="show_post.php">
    2006-06-01<input type="checkbox"
name="dates[20060601]"><br>
    2006-06-02<input type="checkbox"
name="dates[20060602]"><br>
    2006-06-03<input type="checkbox"
name="dates[20060603]"><br>
    2006-06-04<input type="checkbox"
name="dates[20060604]"><br>
    2006-06-05<input type="checkbox"
name="dates[20060605]"><br>
    <input type="submit">
</form></body></html>
```

and I check the boxes next to 2006-06-02 and 2006-06-04 then submit the form, $_POST contains:

```
Array
(
    [dates] => Array
        (
            [20060602] => on
            [20060604] => on
        )

)
```

This script can simply use a foreach() loop through $_POST['dates'] and get all the checked values from the keys of the array.

Question 05: CSS in PHP output (fgetcsv)

I am successfully using "fgetcsv" to parse data from a flat file database into a webpage and wondering whether the output can be formatted using CSS.

The database has only two fields and I would like the first field to have different formatting to the second.

CODE:
```php
<?php
$row = 1;
$handle = fopen("database.csv", "r");
while (($data = fgetcsv($handle, 1000, "|")) !==
FALSE) {
    $num = count($data);

    $row++;
    for ($c=0; $c < $num; $c++) {
        echo $data[$c] . "<br />\n";
    }
}
fclose($handle);
?>
```

Is it possible to format the output using CSS?

A: Place the correct styling before you echo the data. You have this in your code:
```php
. . .
  for ($c=0; $c < $num; $c++) {
      echo $data[$c] . "<br />\n";
  }
. . .
```

All you would need to do is add some html tags, and CSS styling to the echo statement like:

CODE:
```php
. . .
  for ($c=0; $c < $num; $c++) {
```

```
        echo "<span style='color:#FFFFF; ...'" .
$data[$c] . "</span><br />\n";
   }
. . .
```

You can also give the span a class instead of using inline styles.

CODE:
. . .

```
        echo "<span class='myclass'" . $data[$c] ...
```

Question 06: Using a text box for City, State or Zip

I need to determine what has been entered and then parse/pass the values to a web service and/or search query. How can I use a text box for location like City, State or Zip code?

A: U.S. ZIP codes are a 5-digit number optionally followed by a dash and a four-digit number. States have two letters. Anything else could be assumed to be a city name. Try the following:

Use a test form like:
CODE:
```
<html><body>
<form method="post" action="/test_csz.php">
<input type="text" name="value"><input type="submit">
</form></body></html>
```

Or something along the lines of:

CODE:
```php
<?php
if (isset($_POST['value']))
{
    if (preg_match ('/^\d{5}(-\d{4})?$/',
$_POST['value']))
    {
        print 'ZIP code';
    }
    else
    {
        if (preg_match ('/^[a-z]{2}$/i',
$_POST['value']))
        {
            print 'State abbreviation';
        }
        else
        {
            print "assuming it's a city name";
        }
    }
}
?>
```

Question 07: Print all session variables that are currently set

I know we can print a single session variable value by something like:

```
echo "+++".$_SESSION['variable1']."+++";
```

Is it possible to print all session variables and its values (if they have values set) without specifying a particular variable?

A: Yes you can. Use the following:

CODE:

```
print_r ($_SESSION);
```

This will print everything that is in the $_SESSION array.

Question 08: Get part of a string

My script is called like this:

```
script.php?sms=123#456
```

Then I use GET to read $sms into the script.

I would like to retrieve 123 and 456 as two separate values; they can be from 1-5 digits each.

What is the best way to do this?

A: You can use explode(). Check this site for further info:

http://www.php.net/manual/en/function.explode.php

Question 09: Multiple search using PHP

On my site, I have 3 command buttons labeled Google, Yahoo & MSN with 1 'search' text box above.

I am using PHP and would like to be able to press either of the search buttons. I want for it to search from the single text box and then open a new window from that specific search. Is there a way to do this?

A: Yes there is. The new window will have to be opened by the use of the 'target="..."' attribute of the form:

Here's a simple code example:

```php
<?php
$strings = array
(
    'Google' => 'http://www.google.com/search?q=',
    'Yahoo' => 'http://search.yahoo.com/search?p=',
    'MSN' => 'http://search.msn.com/results.aspx?q='
);

if (isset ($_POST['submit_button']))
{
    $query = $strings[$_POST['submit_button']] .
$_POST['search_string'];

    header ('Location: ' . $query);
}
else
{
    print '
<html><body>
<form method="post" action="test_window.php"
target="_new">
<input type="text" name="search_string">
<input type="submit" value="Google"
name="submit_button">
<input type="submit" value="Yahoo"
name="submit_button">
<input type="submit" value="MSN"
name="submit_button">
</form></body></html>';
}
?>
```

Question 10: Creating links from a string

I am putting together a PHP photo gallery and have a field in the mysql database called photoKeywords. This contains some comma delimited keywords for each photo. E.g. Cityname, Countryname, Peoplename

I have created a search page that displays all the photos, captions and keywords that match the search criteria. This works great but I would like to be able to click on a keyword shown beside a photo and rerun the search, finding all the other photos with that keyword.

To do this, I need to change "Cityname, Countryname, Peoplename" into
```
<a
href="viewerTags.php?tag=%25Cityname%25">Cityname</a>
<a
href="viewerTags.php?tag=%25Countryname%25">Countryna
me</a><a
href="viewerTags.php?tag=%25Peoplename%25">Peoplename
</a>
```

I currently use the following code to display the thumbnails:

```php
<?php
    $counter = 0;
    if ($totalRows_thumbs > 0)
    {while($row_thumbs = mysql_fetch_assoc($thumbs)){
        $counter = $counter + 1;
        $thumbs1.= '<div class="comment">';
        $thumbs1.= '</div>';
        $thumbs1.= '<div class="commentmain">';
            $thumbs1.= '<div class="photoinfo">';
                $thumbs1.= 'Photo ID: ' .
$row_thumbs['photoID'] . '<br />';
                $thumbs1.= 'Caption: ' .
$row_thumbs['photoCaption'] . '<br />';
                $thumbs1.= 'Keywords: ' .
$row_thumbs['photoKeywords'] . '<br />';
                $thumbs1.= 'EXIF Info: Hover mouse
over image <br />';
                $thumbs1.= 'Gallery Name: ' .
$row_thumbs['photoGallery'] . '<br /><br />';
```

```
        $thumbs1.= '<a
href="viewerDynamic.php?id=' . $row_thumbs['photoID']
. '&amp;gallery=' . $row_thumbs['photoGallery'] .
'">View large image in original gallery</a>';
        $thumbs1.= '</div>';
        $thumbs1.= '<a href="viewerDynamic.php?id=' .
$row_thumbs['photoID'] . '&amp;gallery=' .
$row_thumbs['photoGallery'] . '"> <img class="image"
src="thumbs/' . $row_thumbs['photoID'] . '" alt="' .
$row_thumbs['photoExif'] . '" title="' .
$row_thumbs['photoExif'] .'"></img></a>';
        $thumbs1.= '</div>';

        };
    }else{
        $thumbs1.= '<br >There are no photos that meet
your criteria.<br />';
        $thumbs1.= 'Please <a href="index.php">try
again</a><br /><br >';
    }
?>
<?php echo $thumbs1; ?>
```

How can I perform the changes I want?

A: Try this:

CODE:
```
// create an array from your keywords
$keyword = split(",",$row_thumbs['photoKeywords'] );
thumbs1.= 'Keywords: ';

// list tag links for each keyword
foreach ($keyword as $word) {
  thumbs1.= "<a
href=\"viewerTags.php?tag=%25{$word}%25\">$word</a>
";
thumbs1.= '<br />';
}
```

Question 11: Headers already sent

I have a page with just the following code in it:

```php
<?php
if ($_COOKIE['company'] == 'HC')
{
header('Location: subscribeto_hc.php');
}
elseif ($_COOKIE['company'] == 'SVC')
{
header('Location: subscribeto_svc.php');
}
else
{
header('Location: subscribeto_sti.php');
}
?>
```

When I bring up this page I get errors like the following below:

Notice: Undefined index: company in
C:\Accounts\stiesaco\wwwRoot\online\subscribeto.php on line
2

Notice: Undefined index: company in
C:\Accounts\stiesaco\wwwRoot\online\subscribeto.php on line
6

Warning: Cannot modify header information - headers already
sent by (output started at
C:\Accounts\stiesaco\wwwRoot\online\subscribeto.php:2) in
C:\Accounts\stiesaco\wwwRoot\online\subscribeto.php on line
12

What is the proper syntax to make this work?

A: The "headers already sent" error will likely go away when you fix the first two.

The problem is that $_COOKIE['company'] is empty. If you attempt to use an uninitialized variable in a PHP conditional, you're going to get that error. Take care of the case where $_COOKIE is empty first, then take care of the rest of the cases:

CODE:
```php
<?php
if (!isset($_COOKIE['company']))
{
    header('Location: subscribeto_sti.php');
}
else
{
    switch ($_COOKIE['company'])
    {
        case 'HC':
            header('Location: subscribeto_hc.php');
            break;
        case 'SVC':
            header('Location: subscribeto_svc.php');
            break;
        default:
            header('Location: subscribeto_sti.php');
    }
}
?>
```

Question 12: Daily Mailing List using PHP/MySQL

I want to make an automatic mailing system that will get information from a MySQL database and send it to a number of subscribers.

I know how to code everything except for one thing: the 'automatic' part. I don't want to go to my website each day and press a 'Send mail' button. What I want is a system which sends the mails itself, e.g. each day at 9 a.m.

Is there a way to do this?

A: If you're using any flavor of UN*X or Linux, use the cron to run your script on a schedule.

On windows you would add a scheduled task (in control panel). The task execution would be "c:/path/to/php.exe c:/path/to/php/script.php". Once the scheduled task is created, right click on it and select advance in order to set more flexible scheduling than the wizard provides.

Question 13: Session based paged listing

I'm currently making a ShoutBox script, which will be quite simple. However, for a paged listing, as far as I know, I would have to run two queries.

One of them would have to check the number of rows to know the limit calculus end.

Example:
CODE:
```
$numrows = mysql_num_rows($get_main);
// how many pages we have when using paging?
$maxPage = ceil($numrows/$limitposts);
```

This has to run after a query and this means that I would have to run two queries.

My idea is to run a query where I retrieve all rows. I put this query in a session array, then simply do a count() on the array and easily generate a paged listing. This will also give less stress on the database as it won't have to run a new query with a new limit for each time.

I know that mysql will "buffer" a bit, but even so, I think the session will give less system stress. It's a small page, and I guess no one will "never" bother to check the other pages in the shoutbox... (shoutbox / guestbook).

* Retrieve all rows, put in session array
* Generate paged listing, based on count ($session_array) and divided on $perpage.

I would have to have some way to "refresh" the session array. What is the best procedure for this?

A: Let's say you have 100 mostly simultaneous users.

Your idea will download the entire database 100 times, and then make 100 copies on the server's filesystem. That doesn't sound like a good idea.

I would do the two queries: one a "SELECT <columnname> ... LIMIT..." query to fetch the limited number of records necessary to populate the page and one a "SELECT count(*) from <tablename>" query to get the number of records.

MySQL optimizes a "SELECT count(*) from <tablename>" query quite well. I remember once reading somewhere on the MySQL site that a query of that type doesn't even check the data in the table. It checks table metadata instead.

And unless you know for a fact that every user will look at every record in your database every time they visit your site, downloading the entire database for every user is counterproductive.

Here is an example of a data-paging script. The "trick" to writing such a script when fetching data from MySQL is to use the "LIMIT" clause of the "SELECT" query. This allows the script to calculate which records to fetch.

The script, as written, uses a table on system that consists of the standard Linux word list ("/usr/share/dict/words"). The table structure can be replicated by the query:

```
CREATE TABLE words
(
    pkID INT UNSIGNED AUTO_INCREMENT PRIMARY KEY,
    word VARCHAR(40) NOT NULL,
    KEY (word)
)
```

The data was loaded into the table using the query:

```
LOAD DATA INFILE '/usr/share/dict/words'
INTO TABLE words (word);
```

This script will display a page of records each time it is run -- the number of records in a page is defined by the variable $records_per_page.

The script expects a value named "page" to be input on the URL. That number denotes which page of $records_per_page records to display. If no input is available on the URL, the script defaults to outputting the first page. If the "page" input variable's value is larger than the maximum possible page size for the given number of $records_per_page, the script will use instead that maximum page size.

The script also provides at the bottom of each display page "previous" and "next" links back to itself with calculated page input values. It will only display these links if doing so is meaningful -- for example, it will not show a "previous" link if it is displaying the first page of data.

In order to get this script to work with your table, you will at a minimum have to:
-modify the $mysql_* variables to match your environment
-change $count_query and $data_query to something meaningful to your database schema and change the print statement in the while loop just below the comment "output the required records" to something meaningful to your table structure.

You may also have to tweak the various table tags output by the code to get everything to line up right.

CODE:
```php
<?php
/* Data paging script
    2006-01-11 by sleipnir214
    This script is in the public domain.

CAUTION: No warranty is expressed or implied as to
how safe it will be for you to use.

    Use this code with trepidation and circumspection.
 */


//variables for connecting to MySQL
$mysql_host = 'localhost';
$mysql_user = 'test';
$mysql_pass = 'test';

$mysql_db   = 'test';
```

```php
//set the number of records per page
$records_per_page = 10;

//connect to MySQL
mysql_connect ($mysql_host, $mysql_user,
$mysql_pass);
mysql_select_db ($mysql_db);
//find out how many records are in the table
$count_query = "SELECT count(*) from words";
$rh = mysql_query ($count_query);
list ($record_count) = mysql_fetch_array($rh);

//calculate the maximum "page" that can be displayed.
$max_pages = floor($record_count /
$records_per_page);

//This logic takes care of reacting to input.
if (isset($_GET['page']))
{
    if ($_GET['page'] > 1)
    {
        if ($_GET['page'] > $max_pages)
        {
            $current_page = $max_pages;
        }
        else
        {
            $current_page = $_GET['page'];
        }
    }
    else
    {
        $current_page = 1;
    }
}
else
{
    $current_page = 1;
}

$limit_start = ($current_page - 1) *
$records_per_page;


//query the database for the required records
$data_query = "SELECT * FROM words LIMIT " .
$limit_start . ", " . $records_per_page;
```

```php
$rh = mysql_query ($data_query);


print '<html><body><table width="100%" border="1">';


//output the required records
while ($word_data = mysql_fetch_array($rh))
{
    print '<tr>';
    print '<td align="center" width="50%">' .
$word_data['pkID'] . '</td>';
    print '<td align="center" width="50%">' .
$word_data['word'] . '</td>';
    print '</tr>';
}


//this is the logic for the "previous" link display
print '<tr><td width="50%" align="center">';
if ($current_page > 1)
{
    print '<a href="' . $_SERVER['PHP_SELF'] .
'?page=' . ($current_page - 1) . '">previous</a>';
}
else
{
    print ' ';
}
print '</td>';


//this is the logic for the "next" link display
print '<td width="50%" align="center">';
if ($limit_start + $records_per_page < $record_count)
{
    print '<a href="' . $_SERVER['PHP_SELF'] .
'?page=' . ($current_page + 1) . '">next</a>';
}
else
{
    print ' ';
}
print '</td></tr></table><body></html>';
?>
```

Question 14: Getting multiple fields from a POST form

Here is what I'm trying to do and the corresponding status:

1 - Pull multiple fields from a database, these fields are all similar - got this done.

2 - Display it as an html form for updating - got this done.

3 - Submit the changed/updated information back to the database. This is where I'm having problems. Let's say I'm updating the field named "name" in the database. So for example, I have a form with 5 fields and they all are named "name". I can also pull the "name_id" from the database, which is unique, if that is needed.

Now the problem that I'm facing is after the form is submitted. How do I go through all of the "name" fields and update them in the database to reflect the changes?

A: There is a little-known, obscurely-documented feature of PHP that might be of help here.

If you have multiple fields of the same name, then name them as if they were PHP arrays:

```
<form method="post"....>
<input type="text" name="person_name[1]"><br>
<input type="text" name="person_name[2]"><br>
<input type="text" name="person_name[3]"><br>
<input type="text" name="person_name[4]"><br>
<input type="text" name="person_name[5]"><br>
.
.
.
</form>
```

Then $_POST['person_name'] will itself be an array. If your database has a field which records a unique ID for each record, you can use those as the subscripts in the field names in your form. That way, all you have to do is use a while() loop across the values in $_POST['person_name'] and have the IDs to use in your UPDATE queries.

And additional thing to do is to store the original data in a hidden field:

```
<form method="post"...>
<input type="text" name="person_name[1]">
<input type="text"
name="origonal_person_name[1]"><br>
<input type="text" name="person_name[2]">
<input type="text"
name="origonal_person_name[2]"><br>
<input type="text" name="person_name[3]">
<input type="text"
name="origonal_person_name[3]"><br>
<input type="text" name="person_name[4]">
<input type="text"
name="origonal_person_name[4]"><br>
<input type="text" name="person_name[5]">
<input type="text"
name="origonal_person_name[5]"><br>
.
.
.
</form>
```

This way, your script can compare the field with what was originally stored and change only those records in the database which the user changes. You could also store the original field data in session variables.

Use this code to break it up and insert it back into the database:
CODE:
```
foreach($arrayname as $key=>$value)
    {
    echo $key.": ".$value;
    ***SQL CODE HERE
    }
```

Question 15: Convert HTML code into Text

I have used file ($url) as a way to grab a webpage. I am interested in knowing how to turn that code into true HTML code in text format instead of activated HTML. For instance, I might pull off a link form a website and it will show up when displayed from a variable like so:

CODE:
```
Active link
```

Instead of:

CODE:
```
<a href="http://www.site.com">Non Active Link</a>
```

How can I convert HTML code into text format?

A: Try running the content of the website contents through htmlentities().

PHP Manual entry for htmlentities:

http://www.php.net/manual/en/function.htmlentities.php

Then you can just echo it, and it should look normal, but will not get parsed by the browser.

Question 16: debug_backtrace( ) safely

I would like to print debug_backtrace( ) to the screen every time an error occurs. I know how to do it but my question then becomes, is it safe? Would providing that kind of information allow a hacker to take a whack at the erroneous script?

A: No user should ever see anything but what you want him to see. A user does not need to see the debug_backtrace() output, so I recommend that you not show it to him.

However, there is nothing to stop you from outputting that data to a log file and printing an error message which includes a "click back and try again; if you get this error message a second time, email this page to...error page". Your script could then output a time/date stamp that will lead you to the place in the log file where the error occurred.

You could also have the script email you the debug_backtrace() output directly.

Don't show that information to users.

Question 17: Parsing a page element

I am trying to get link popularity from Google and haven't been able to isolate the section I need. Perhaps my regex is wrong or something else, but I've been experimenting with everything and cannot seem to grab the line with results.

Take a look:
CODE:

```
function getlp($url) {
    $file =
"http://www.google.com/search?hl=en&lr=&ie=UTF-
8&q=link%3A$url";
    $data = file($file);
    $trans="";
    preg_match_all("/[of]\s[about]\s[0-
9\,]*\s[linking]\s[to]/Ui", $data[34], $regs);
    $trans=get_html_translation_table(HTML_ENTITIES);
    $result=strtr($regs[0][0], $trans);
    return $result;
}
```

How can I successfully isolate the section I need?

A: I found this pattern to work with your code:

CODE:

```
/of\sabout\s<b>[0-9,]+<\/b>\slinking\sto/Ui
```

When run your function returns: "of about 3,050,000 linking to"
Obviously the number is arbitrary...

One thing, when writing the pattern the html code is contained in the string $data[34], so the pattern must account for
....

Question 18: Arrays not acknowledging white space

The following code displays an array (value format: aaa bbb) in a list box with the correct values but when the OK button is selected, it submits the values back onto the page but fails to recognize the 2nd part of each value of the array (i.e. bbb). I'm sure this is down to the white space within the values of the array.

CODE:
```
<html>
<script language="JavaScript">
function SelectAll(combo)
  {
    for (var i=0;i<combo.options.length;i++)
    {
      combo.options[i].selected=true;
    }
  }
</script>
<body><form name="form" action="<?php echo
$_SERVER["PHP_SELF"]; ?>" method="post">
<?php
        $CorrectArray = array("aaa bbb","ccc
ddd","eee fff","ggg hhh");

        echo '<select name="auswahl[]" multiple>';
        foreach($CorrectArray as $ValueArray
=>$Answer)
        {
            echo "<option value=$Answer\n>$Answer\n";
        }
        echo '</select><br /><br />';
?>
<input type="submit" value="OK"
onclick="SelectAll(document.form.elements['auswahl[]'
])">
</form>
<?php
        $auswahl = $_POST["auswahl"];

          echo '<pre>';
        print_r($_POST);
        echo '</pre>';
  ?>
```

33

```
</body></html>
```

How can I get it to read the whole value (i.e. aaa bbb)?

A: If the value attributes of form inputs have white space, those values must be inside quotes. You were not doing that.

This line should be:
```
echo "<option value=$Answer>$Answer\n";
```

should read something like:
```
echo '<option value="' . $Answer . '">' . $Answer . "\n";
```

It's a good idea to get into the habit of using quotes all the time.

Question 19: Date Drop Down format issue

CODE:

```php
function DateDropDown(){
    echo '<select name="MM">';
    for ($i = 1; $i <= 12; $i++){
        echo '<option value="';
        printf('%0-2d', $i);
        echo '">';
        printf('%0-2d', $i);
        echo '</option>';
    }
    echo '</select>/';
    echo '<select name="DD">';
    for ($i = 1; $i <= 31; $i++){
        echo '<option value="';
        printf('%0-2d', $i);
        echo '">';
        printf('%0-2d', $i);
        echo '</option>';
    }
    echo '</select>/';
    echo '<select name="YYYY">';
    for ($i = 2005; $i <= 2010; $i++){
        echo '<option value="';
        printf('%0-2d', $i);
        echo '">';
        printf('%0-2d', $i);
        echo '</option>';
    }
    echo '</select>';
```

I need the day and the month to have the leading 0 as in 01/01/2005 so that I can use it as a legit date data type for mysql database in the form YYYYMMDD.
What is the necessary step to do this?

A: I think the minimum necessary change is to modify every instantiation of:

```
%0-2d
to
%02d
```

Question 20: Method of calling phpBB functions

I have been teaching myself PHP for a while now and finally at a stage where I am trying to put together a web forum written from scratch in PHP. I have been reading the phpBB code to try and understand everything that it does so that I can include as much functionality in my own forum as possible (I don't want to just copy and paste though, I want to understand it).

I repeatedly keep running into a piece of code which appears to be calling a function from the template.php page, yet I don't understand why it works (I come from an ASP background, so it could just be a clash of understanding).

The function in includes/template.php:

CODE:
```php
function set_filenames($filename_array)
{
    if (!is_array($filename_array))
    {
        return false;
    }
    reset($filename_array);
    while(list($handle, $filename) =
each($filename_array))
    {
        $this->files[$handle] = $this-
>make_filename($filename);
    }
return true;
}
```
How it is called in posting.php:

CODE:
```php
$template->set_filenames(array(
    'confirm_body' => 'confirm_body.tpl')
);
```

Why is this calling the function since it has $template on the front? What is the meaning of the '->' is?

A: The function set_filenames() is inside a class. It is a method of an object which you have called $template. I suspect that somewhere above this line there is a statement similar to:

require_once template.php;
$template = new HTML_TEMPLATE;

Thus, the -> operator is an object assignment operator.

Search Google or PHP.net for object oriented programming to get a fuller understanding. Most people find objects a neat way of doing things.

Question 21: Variable using current_date function

I want to say so many days left till The Event. The distance to the time is current date – 2006-03-31.

Is there a way to declare a variable $to_event for instance and use it with an echo?

A: The code below will do what you want. It ignores whether the event is in the past or the future. You can change this by getting rid of the "abs" in the second line of get_time_diff.

CODE:
```
$to_event = get_time_diff("2006-03-31", "format");
echo "<pre>";
print_r "$to_event";
echo "</pre>";

function get_time_diff($date, $format="seconds") {
  $datestamp = strtotime($date);
  $seconds = abs(strtotime("now") - $datestamp);
  if($format === "seconds"):
    return array("seconds"=>$seconds);
  else:
    return time_format($seconds);
  endif;
}
function time_format($seconds) {
  $seconds = (float) $seconds;
  $secs = round((($seconds/60)-floor($seconds/60)) *
60,1);
  $mins = floor((($seconds/3600)-
floor($seconds/(3600))) *60) ;
  $hrs = floor((($seconds/(3600*24))-
floor($seconds/(3600*24))) *24) ;
  $days = floor($seconds / (3600*24));
  $days = ($days<0) ? 0 : $days;
  return  array("days"=>$days, "hours"=>$hours,
"mins"=>$minutes, "seconds"=>$seconds);
}
```

The format code is written in case you wanted the output as days, hours, minutes and seconds (as people often do).

The actual time difference (in seconds) can be achieved by just the following: (where $date is something like "2006-03-21")

CODE:
```
$seconds = abs(strtotime("now") - strtotime($date));
```

For additional information:
See PHP Manual, Part IV, Function Reference, Date and Time functions. It's time() function. See also mktime() function (convert year-month-day in int seconds) in the same part then subtract two int values (in seconds).

Question 22: File upload error

I have an input=file object on the form called pix.
The file uploads but the script below just won't update the
record.

```
$picturequery = "UPDATE adds SET
picture={$_FILES['pix']['name']} where
accountno=$_POST[record]";

$pictureresult = mysql_query($picturequery) or die
("Couldn't execute the Update picture Query.");
```

My mysql table field is called picture and the type is
varchar(255). The table row already exists and I am just trying to
update the record part of the table row.

I also have another form to upload when creating the initial
record. This creates the whole row; it inserts the picture name
with no problem.

I did attempt to use a text field to update the row with a string of
text i.e. image.gif but also failed. What measures should be done
to correct this error?

A: Get some better debugging.

Change:

```
$pictureresult = mysql_query($picturequery) or die
("Couldn't execute the Update picture Query.");
```

To:

```
$pictureresult = mysql_query($picturequery) or die
(mysql_error());
```

It has something to do with missing single quotes around strings
in a query but that error output should tell you exactly.

Question 23: Count a particular word appearing in a text

Let's say I have the following string/text:

`$text= "new day new problem."`

How can I count the word "new" and how many times it appears? It could also be in two words, like "new day".

A: Try the substr_count() The PHP online manual at php.net.

Quote (PHP Manual):

substr_count() returns the number of times the needle substring occurs in the haystack string. Please note that needle is case sensitive.

Example:

CODE:
```
$text = 'This is a test';
echo substr_count($text, 'is'); // 2
```

It finds the substring "is" 2 times in the original string.

Question 24: Two values in the value property

Here is my current script:

CODE:
```
<input name=\"planyr\" type=\"radio\" value=\"$one\"
checked=\"checked\" />1 Year Extended Warranty Plan
(<strong>$one dollars</strong>)
```

It gets data from a row which has prices for 1, 2 and 3 years and displays them in three option boxes with their prices as the values.

I want to pass how many years they have selected along with the price when they submit the form so that I can enter them into two separate fields; let's say price and year.

I was thinking if I can use something like:

```
checkbox 1 = value=1$one
checkbox 2 = value=2$two
checkbox 3 = value=3$three
```

Where in the first digit will be considered as the years and from the 2nd digit till the end would be considered as the price. How can I do this in PHP?

A: It might be better to put the number of years in a session variable or in a hidden field on the form. But you can do what you ask:

CODE:
```
<input name=\"planyr\" type=\"radio\"
value=\"1_$one\" checked=\"checked\" />1 Year
Extended Warranty Plan (<strong>$one
dollars</strong>)
```

Then parse the incoming value;

CODE:
```
function parsevalue($val) {
  $years = substr($val, 0,1);
  $value = substr($val, 2);
  return array("years"=>$years, "value"=>$val);
}
```

Question 25: PHP doesn't recognize mysql

I've installed both php and mysql. Both seem to work okay but I cannot get php to list mysql in the phpinfo page. I have changed the extensions dir path and uncommented the php_mysql.dll line in php.ini. I've ensured that it is indeed referencing the correct php.ini file and have rebooted. How can I run this correctly?

A: Run a script which consists entirely of:

```
<?php
phpinfo ();
?>
```

Then check the output for "extension_dir".

Question 26: Format month

I want to convert number 4 to month of April. I've tried strftime function but it accepts the full date not just a number.

```
strftime("%B", $date);
```

How can I convert a single number into a month?

A: The easiest way is to make an array with all months.

CODE:
```
$months = array(
    'January', 'February', 'March', 'April', 'May',
'June',
    'July', 'August', 'September', 'October',
'November', 'December'
);

$monthID = 4;

echo $months[$monthID - 1];
```

Question 27: $_POST is null

If I try to post a form which is placed on two different pages with the same action-page, the strings return null in IE but not in Firefox.

Page a:

HTML Code:

```
<form name='form2' method='post' action='addlog.php'>
  <table width='100%' border='0' cellspacing='0'
cellpadding='0'>
    <tr>
      <td align='center' width='33%'>Dato</td>
      <td width='33%' align='center'>Aktivitet</td>
      <td width='33%' align='center'>Varighed
(timer)</td>
    </tr>
    <tr>
      <td align='center'><input name='dato'
type='textfield' size='22' value='<?php echo
"".$date_array['mday']."/".$date_array['mon']."-
".$date_array['year'].""; ?>'></td>
      <td width='33%' align='center'><input
name='aktivitet' type='textfield' size='22'></td>
      <td width='33%' align='center'><input
name='varighed' type='textfield' size='22'></td>
    </tr>
    <tr>
      <td colspan='3' align='right'><input
type='submit' name='Submit2'
value='Tilf&oslash;j'></td>
    </tr>
  </table>
  <p align='right'>  </p>
</form>

Page b:
HTML Code:
<form name='form2' method='post' action='addlog.php'>
  <table width='100%' border='0' cellspacing='0'
cellpadding='0'>
    <tr>
      <td align='center' width='33%'>Dato</td>
```

```
<td width='33%' align='center'>Aktivitet</td>
<td width='33%' align='center'>Varighed
(timer)</td>
    </tr>
    <tr>
    <td align='center'><input name='dato'
type='text' size='22' value='<?php echo
"".$date_array['mday']."/".$date_array['mon']."-
".$date_array['year']."";  ?>'></td>
    <td width='33%' align='center'><input
name='aktivitet' type='text' size='22'></td>
    <td width='33%' align='center'><input
name='varighed' type='text' size='22'></td>
    </tr>
    <tr>
    <td colspan='3' align='right'><input
type='submit' name='Submit2'
value='Tilf&oslash;ji'></td>
    </tr>
  </table>
  <p align='right'>  </p>
</form>
```

Processing page:
PHP Code:
```
<?php
include('isuser.php');
include('config.php');
// connect to the mysql database server.
mysql_connect ($dbhosti, $dbusernameii, $dbuserpass);
mysql_select_db($dbname) or die("Cannot select
database");

$tdato = $_POST["dato"];
$taktivitet = $_POST["aktivitet"];
$tvarighed = $_POST["varighed"];
$username = $_SESSION["s_usernamei"];

if(!isset($tdato)||!isset($taktivitet)||!isset($tvarigh
ed)) {
echo "
<script language='javascript' type='text/javascript'>
        alert('Du har ikke udfyldt alle felter!');
        top.location.replace('logbog.php');
</script>
<noscript>
<META HTTP-EQUIV='REFRESH' CONTENT='0;logbog.php'>
</noscript>";
```

```
}else{
$query="INSERT INTO $username (`dato` , `aktivitet` ,
`varighed` )
VALUES ('$tdato', '$taktivitet', '$tvarighed')";
mysql_query($query) or die(mysql_error());
echo "<META HTTP-EQUIV='REFRESH'
CONTENT='0;logbog.php'>";
}
?>
```

A: You're all backwards. Use single quotes for strings in PHP and double quotes for attributes in HTML.

Question 28: MySQL and deleting rows

If I try to delete e.g. row 2:

Id text:
1) 1 test
2) 2 test
3) 3 test

MySQL leaves behind row 1 & 3. I need row 3 (and all after this) to jump down one number in id. It does not matter where in the table it is necessary.

I need to preserve all records and with id's in the correct order. If I try to loop some echoing (echo the values of the table), it just goes crazy.

Example:
[php] . . .

```php
$row = mysql_num_rows($query);
while($n<$row){
echo "Some content";
$n=$n+1;
}
```

When MySQL encounters "missing" id's (1, 2, 3, 5 ...), it just echoes blank and continues;

Is there a possible solution to this?

A: Use mysql_fetch_row().

PHP Code:
```php
while($row=mysql_fetch_array($result))
{
    //do stuff
}
```

Question 29: Something with Query Strings

In querystrings you always have something like this:

Code:

```
page.php?start=10&offset=5&category=45
```

But in some cases, I see the querystring like this

Code:

```
page.php?start=10;offset=5;category=45
```

Replacing the Amperand - & with a semi-colon - ;

How is this done? How do you read out the querystring values?

A: All querystring parameters are stored in the $_GET[] superglobal* array. The parameter delimeter can be set in php.ini, if you really want, but it is immaterial if you use $_GET.

PHP Code:
```
$start = $_GET['start'];
```

Etc.

Remember if you use GET parameters in SQL queries, to always ensure they are secured. For example, casting to a number for numeric parameters, and enclosing string parameters in quotes.

So if you were to use 'start' in a SQL query, you would do this:

PHP Code:
```
$start = (int) $_GET['start'];
```


If you pass this querystring:
Code:
```
start=10&offset=5&category=45
```

and your delimiter is set as '&' (which is default), you can access
each parameter like this:

PHP Code:
```
$start = $_GET['start'];
$offset = $_GET['offset'];
$category = $_GET['category'];
```

etc.

If you have this querystring:
Code:
```
start=10;offset=5;category=45
```

and the delimiter is set as ';', the same PHP code will yield the
same result.

Furthermore, there is a setting which can be set in the php.ini file
called arg_separator.input. If you don't have access to the
php.ini file, you can access the query string through
$_SERVER['QUERY_STRING'] and use explode to set up your
array:

PHP Code:
```
<?php

function parse_custom_query_string($arg_separator =
';', $value_separator = '=')
{
    $_GET = array(); // clear old $_GET array

    /* separate query string using the arg_separator
*/
    $pairs = explode($arg_separator,
$_SERVER['QUERY_STRING']);

    /* loop through each name value pair */
    foreach($pairs as $value) {

        /* ignore if no value separator is present */
        if (($pos = strpos($value, $value_separator))
=== false) {
            continue;
        }
```

```
        /* extract and decode each component */
        $name = urldecode(substr($value, 0, $pos));
        $value = urldecode(substr($value, $pos +1));

        /* add to the $_GET array */
        $_GET[$name] = $value;
    }
}

parse_custom_query_string();
?>
```

Question 30: Reading email with PHP

I know you can use PHP to send emails but can you use PHP to read incoming emails? Is it a question of manipulating the directory where the emails are being received on the server?

A: Use the IMAP() functions. They are fairly easy to use once you get the hang of them.

Here's a small program I just wrote to read a POP mailbox and insert records into a MySQL table.

CODE:

```
$user = 'xxxx'; // pop3 user name
$pwd = 'xxxx';  // pop3 password
$hst = 'example.com'; // host address
$mbox = imap_open ('{'.$hst.':110/pop3}INBOX', $user,
$pwd);
$headers = imap_headers($mbox);
if (imap_num_msg($mbox) == 0) exit();
// Include MySQL database information
$connect = mysql_connect($dbhost, $dbuser, $dbpassi)
or die ("Unable to connect!");
$db = mysql_select_db($dbname);

for ($i = 1; $i <= imap_num_msg($mbox); $i++)
{
    $qtmpi = array();
    $header = imap_headerinfo($mbox, $i, 80, 80);
    $msg_date = $header->Date;
    $from = $header->from;
    foreach ($from as $id => $object) {
        $fromname = $object->personal;
        $fromaddress = $object->mailbox . "@" .
$object->host;
    }i
//    $qtmp[] =  ($qtmp will be used to create the
query
    $messageBody = imap_body($mbox, $i);
    $tmp = explode(',',$messageBody);
    $q = 'insert into mysql_table set ';
    $q .= implode(',',$qtmp);
    echo $q."\n";
    mysql_query($q) or die(mysql_error());
    imap_delete($mbox,$i);
```

```
   }
imap_expunge($mbox);
imap_close($mbox);
?>
```

Some of the above code comes directly from php.net

Question 31: Make virtual directory in Apache

I installed apache in my c drive under c:\webserver\apache\ and my public directory where I put my html files which are all located at c:\webserver\public\

I got a huge list of files outside the web server and are located at c:\folder\filename\myfiles. I want to make my website point to that folder and use these folders' content without having to move them inside my public apache folder.

Is there a way to make it like http:\localhost\myfiles and be able to access c:\folder\filename\myfiles without having to move the folder inside the web server?

A: You can change the root directory or you can take one of my virtual hosts and use it as an example:

Quote:
```
<VirtualHost *:80>
ServerName natesblog.us.to
DocumentRoot "/Program Files/Apache
Group/Apache2/htdocs/blog"
ServerAlias www.natesblog.us.to
</VirtualHost>
```

Servername is the name you want to name it (I believe this can be anything), DocumentRoot (obvious), and ServerAlias is where you put the URL to that site (use a space for multiple urls like "www.natesblog.us.to natesblog.us.to").

Question 32: Make script of mysql database using phpmyadmin

I want to transfer a copy of my database tables and data to a different machine and use it as a backup. How can I make a backup of my mysql database using phpmyadmin?

A: Within phpmyadmin, in the navigation on the left, click the database name.
Then after the page loads, there should be a tab across the top "Export". Click it.
Select All Tables. Fill out the rest of the form and be sure to save to file. Include whatever options you want and click the appropriate button.

When you export be sure to choose compatibility as "Mysql 4" and add the options +drop database and +use statement.

Question 33: Finding out an Autonumber

I'm using odbc and got a php script that does a simple insert into an MS Access table that has a field 'SpecID' set as an Autonumber. Is there a way of getting the SpecID number either before or after the new record is created?

A: You will need to execute another query, at the very least;

http://www.utteraccess.com/forums/s...1086320&fpart=1

Using standard compliant SQL, you can do this:

Code:

```
SELECT MAX(id) AS last_id FROM table_name;
```

Question 34: Writing "last modified" on my page

I want to add a "Last Modified..." on my index page. I know how to get the last modified date of an actual file but I would really like to do it with the main folder (www) where all my files are in; since my index page won't change but the folder always will, with new data and such.

Does anyone know how to display the last modified date of the topmost folder? On my server, it's the www folder.

A: Try this code:

```php
<?php
    // This gets the last modified date of the
root directory (www)
        $filename = $_SERVER[DOCUMENT_ROOT];
        if (file_exists($filename)) {
            $modDatei = date ("F d Y H:i:s.",
filemtime($filename));
        }
?>
```

Question 35: @ and & in PHP

I have seen object declaration like $db = &new DB. What does @ and & means in PHP?

A: The @ character is the error suppression operator. It is equivalent to calling the error_reporting(0) before and after the statement. In effect, it prevents PHP from spitting out any notices, warnings or fatal error messages. It DOES NOT however, make the error go away, fatal errors still kill the script and warnings or notices which would once be displayed may go unnoticed. You should use the error suppression operator in conjunction with a check, i.e.:

PHP Code:
```
if (! ($fhwnd = fopen('blah', 'r')) {
    /* file failed to open */

}
```

The above statement attempts to open a file, if it fails the code inside the If statement is executed. The error suppression operator is used to prevent PHP from displaying the warning message generated if it does fail.

The character "&" is the variable reference operator. In PHP a variable identifier: i. e.: $foo, is a name used to identify a specific location in memory. This location will contain a value. Sometimes, it may be necessary to have several identifiers which point to the same location. This is especially the case with objects and arrays; most languages in fact, including PHP 5+, use references by default for objects.

In contrast to a normal variable identifier, in a reference, the variable name instead refers to a location in memory, which contains another location in memory. When we refer to a referenced variable, PHP looks up that location and fetches the value from there.

PHP Code:
```
$variable1 = 'hello';
```

```
$reference1 = &$variable1;
$variable2 = $variable1;
$reference2 = &$variable1;

echo($variable1); // outputs hello
$reference2 = 'goodbye'; // this changes $reference1
to a variable
echo($variable2); // outputs hello

$variable1 = "goodbye";

echo($reference1); // outputs goodbye
```

As you can see, a change to the variable causes this change to be reflected by all variables that hold a reference to it, as they all refer to the same location. Unfortunately, PHP does not have a dereference operator, so it is not possible to update the real variable via the reference.

In PHP 4, arrays and objects are always assigned by value, that means that if you create an object and assign it to another variable, all its data is copied into a new location in memory. For objects in particular this behavior (known as cloning) is rarely required and can lead to problems, for example, cloning an object in PHP 4 causes its constructor to be called again on the new instance.

It is for this reason that in PHP 4 objects are often created as follow:

PHP Code:
```
$ref = &new ObjectName;
```

Now, when the object is assigned to another variable:

PHP Code:
```
$ref2 = $ref;
```

This too, will hold a reference to the same object.

As of PHP 5, you need to worry about this as all objects are passed by reference as default.

Question 36: Retain original value from PASSWORD

I want to retain back the original value of a variable $pass that was inserted in the database like this:

```
mysql_query("INSERT INTO table1 SET username =
'$name', password = PASSWORD('$pass'));
```

I would like to call the field value into a form that only accepts 8 characters. When it was encrypted and called through <input type= "password" name = "pass" value= "$row[$pass]">, it returns more than 8 characters that give my code errors.

How to retain original value from PASSWORD($pass)?

A: Basically, you cannot.

It is also a better practice to set the password fields to a string like 'unchanged' (or perhaps something less likely to be chosen by your users) and check for a changed value from within the formhandler. If the value is different from the string you used as the default value, then it's changed by the user. If it is the same, don't update the password to the record.

If you want to offer your users an "I forgot my password" function, you'll be better of by creating a new password and mailing it to your user.

Question 37: Take content from another site

I know about RSS and want to use a database to store some information. How can I take content from another site? What book can I use to learn this?

A: You can use curl or even file_get_contents in combination with regular expressions to extract the desired information.

Check this out:
http://in.php.net/curl

Question 38: Bug in URL decoding

Consider the following script:

```php
<?php
foreach ( $_GET as $key => $value ) {
print ("$key=$value<br>");
}
$value = '"foobar"'; // I need to pass " in the HTTP
query.
print ("value=".$value."<br>"); // prints out
value="foobar"
print ("<a
href='".$_SERVER['SCRIPT_NAME'].'?value='.urlencode($
value). "'>click me to see the bug</a>");
%>
```

I need to pass a value in HTTP query containing a quote (").

When I run this script with "?value=foobar" query string, everything works fine and it prints:
`value=foobar`.

When I run this script with "?value=%22foobar%22" query string (passing '"foobar"' instead of just 'foobar'), then the script prints out:
`value=\"foobar\"`

Where does it get the \ from? It should be just value="foobar".

Is this a bug or is there some setting in PHP that can change this behavior?

A: Read out these lines which I got from the PHP manual.

"The PHP directive magic_quotes_gpc is on by default, and it essentially runs addslashes() on all GET, POST, and COOKIE data"

addslashes() function will escape the double quotes. This is the reason for the presence of slashes in your output.
In the php.ini file just set the directive 'magic_quotes_gpc' to 'off' and you will get the desired output.

Question 39: Get name initials

CODE:

```php
<?php
function get_initials($name) {
$name = strtolower($name);
$name = explode(' ', $name);
foreach($name as $key => $value)
{
$initials = $name[$key][0];
echo $initials;
}
return ;
}
?>
<?php
$date = date("my");
$test_string = "Mylene salviejo corporation";
$initialized = get_initials($test_string);
$sellerIDdb = $initialized . $date;
//echo $sellerIDdb;
if (!empty($sellerIDdb))
{
header ("Location: index.php");
exit();
}
?>
```

I am getting this error:

"msc
Warning: Cannot modify header information - headers already
sent by (output started at C:\Program Files\Abyss Web
Server\htdocs\charity\intiials.php:8) in C:\Program Files\Abyss
Web Server\htdocs\charity\intiials.php on line 22"

Output started at line 8 means the code is reading my function. If
I remove the echo on my function it will not return the exact
initials I am producing for each loop. It will just output: c instead
of msc.

If values can be handled by a variable then I can insert that easily
in the database without echoing. Thus my header redirection will
push through.

Is there a good variable handler for the "$initials = $name[$key][0]; >>"?

A: You cannot have echo $initials; in your function. This is outputting data before the headers are sent. Return a string from the function and save that, then output the string if it doesn't need to do the header redirect.

If however you are trying to output the initials on the screen and do the redirect, this is not possible. You will need to do the outputting on the index.php screen after the redirect has occurred. You can pass some get variables in your header redirect to help trigger this.

Here is how it should look assuming you only want to output if the header redirect does not happen.

```php
<?php
function get_initials($name) {
$name = strtolower($name);
$name = explode(' ', $name);
$initials = ""
foreach($name as $key => $value)
{
$initials .= $name[$key][0];

}
return $initials;
}

$date = date("my");
$test_string = "Mylene salviejo corporation";
$initialized = get_initials($test_string);
$sellerIDdb = $initialized . $date;
//echo $sellerIDdb;
if (!empty($sellerIDdb))
{
header ("Location: index.php");
exit();
}
else
{
echo $initialized;
}
?>
```

Question 40: Whitespace

I'm using PHP and its OO model. I've started building a system which has a pretty large projected audience. Keeping that in mind, I'm trying to make sure I am programming their system as expandable and optimized as I possibly can.

Recently, I've been getting into keeping better formatted code using extra tabs and spaces between variables, operators, and semi-colons.

For example:
```php
<?php
$DB         = new DBConnect();

$id         = 209990;
$fname      = "John";
$lname      = "Apple";
$email      = "johnapple@email_provider.com";
$address    = "1234 Smithe Street, Miami, FL, 33102";

$selQ       = 'UPDATE #__TblProfile SET
                    fname   = "'.$DB-
>real_escape($fname).'",
                    lname   = "'.$DB-
>real_escape($lname).'",
                    email   = "'.$DB-
>real_escape($email).'",
                    address = "'.$DB-
>real_escape($address).'"
                WHERE id    = '.$id.'
                LIMIT 1';
$selQ       = $DB->setQuery($selQ);
/* OUTPUTS:
UPDATE COMTblProfile SET
  fname   = "John",
  lname   = "Apple",
  email   = "johnapple@email_provider.com",
  address = "1234 Smithe Street, Miami, FL, 33102"
  WHERE id = 209990
  LIMIT 1
*/
($DB->query($selQ)) || die($DB->FailedQuery($selQ));
$DB->close();
?>
```

Is it bad to have so many spaces, usually tabs, as I did? Does it affect the processing speed of either PHP or MySQL?

A: Whitespace will not affect your processing speed.

Use it to make your code easier to read not only for yourself but also for people who may have to modify your code.

When the script is read in, all whitespace is ignored. It takes absolutely no processing power unless you are sticking in a couple thousand spaces per line and even then the amount of processing power would be so infinitesimal that maybe 1/1000000th of a second may have passed.

Question 41: Cannot read variable on php5

I have a database named abcd and a simple table named table1 like this on mysql:

```
+---------+-------------+----------------+
| id(int) | name(char)  | comment(text)  |
+---------+-------------+----------------+
| 1 | abe | bla bla bla |
| 2 | bob | blo blo blo |
| 3 | joe | bli bli bli |
+---------+-------------+----------------+
```

And a following script;

test.php

```php
<?php

mysql_connect("localhost", "username", "password");
mysql_select_db("abcd");

$query=mysql_query("SELECT * FROM table1");

$num=mysql_num_rows($query);
echo($num."<br><br>");

while($row=mysql_fetch_array($query))
{
echo("<a
href=detail.php?id=$row[id]>".$row[name]."</a>"."<br
");
}

?>
```

detail.php

```php
<?php

mysql_connect("localhost", "username", "password");
mysql_select_db("abcd");
```

```
$query=mysql_query("SELECT * FROM table1 WHERE id =
'$id' ");

$num=mysql_num_rows($query);
echo("record selected : ".$num."<br><br>");

$row=mysql_fetch_array($query);
echo($row[name]."<br>"."<i>".$row[comment]."</i>");

?>
```

When I click link abe to see his comment, the browser shows me
this page:
```
-----------------------------+
record selected : 0 |
|
| <- monitor screen
|
|
-----------------------------+
```

Instead of:

```
-----------------------------+
record selected : 1 |
|
abe | <- monitor screen
<I>bla bla bla</I> |
|
-----------------------------+
```

but when I change;

```
...
$query=mysql_query("SELECT * FROM table1 WHERE id =
'$id' ");
...
```

to

```
...
$query=mysql_query("SELECT * FROM table1 WHERE id = 1
");
...
```

It works for abe but not for the others (bob and john) because its id will always refer to abe.

I know it sounds ridiculous because the book which I read says that it should work fine, so where did I go wrong then?

I'm using php5 with apache 2.x and mysql 5.x. At first I think maybe I messed with the configuration so I uninstalled that software from my computer and try to use xammp which do the configuration automatically, but it still happen. Then I try to install the xammp on a different computer and the problem is still occurred.

How can I solve this problem?

A: The problem is probably that register_globals is turned off, what is by default in php installation and recommended. So your $id variable is not automatically created from GET variables in your detail.php.

You can access your variable through $_GET array
```
$id = $_GET['id'];
// do query...
```

Or set register_globals on at php.ini file.

Question 42: Session Variables Lost

In my application, the user goes through a series of forms. If the information was posted in the previous form, I can access it through the $_POST['variablename'] convention. However, because I need to access information that was entered several forms earlier; I decided to use SESSION variables. This is also useful because I don't want to store this information for longer than the user is at the site.

While I can access the $_SESSION['variablename'] on the page where it was assigned, I cannot access it later on another page. This seems to defeat the purpose of SESSION variables.

Here is the code for two pages. The assignment of values to $_SESSION['CandidateName0'] works as I can output the values from when I am on the first page. However, I cannot output them in the second.

```
_____ENTER CRITERIA PAGE STARTS_____
<?php
// initialize a session
session_start();
?>
<html>
<head> <title>Enter Criteria</title> </head>
<body>

<?php
//Candidate Name was posted in previous page
$_SESSION['CandidateName0'] =
$_POST['CandidateName0'];
$_SESSION['CandidateName1'] =
$_POST['CandidateName1'];
$_SESSION['CandidateName2'] =
$_POST['CandidateName2'];
$_SESSION['CandidateName3'] =
$_POST['CandidateName3'];
$_SESSION['CandidateName4'] =
$_POST['CandidateName4']; //Assignment works I can
output $_SESSION variables here
?>

<form method="post" action="EnterRankings.php">
<h3>Enter most important criteria: </h3>
```

```
<select name="CriteriaName0">
<option value="Cost">Cost
<option value="Near Schools">Near schools
</select>
<br/> <br/>
<input type="submit" value="Continue To Rankings">
</form>

</body>
</html>
```

_____EnterRankings.php STARTS_____

```
<html>
<head></head>
<body>
<?php
echo $_SESSION['CandidateName0'];
//This is what doesn't work!!!
?>

<?php echo $_POST['CriteriaName0']; ?>
//But I can access variables from the POST
// in the previous page

</body>
</html>
```

I went through http://www.zend.com/php/beginners/php101-10.php tutorial on SESSION variables and everything worked fine so it seems my system is set up correctly. What am I doing wrong?

A: First, allow me to point out that you really should pre-process your POST and GET data prior to assigning (in case you forget later).

For instance:

```
$var = ($_POST['var']) ? (int)$_POST['var'] : NULL;
$str = ($_POST['str']) ? addslashes($_POST['str']) :
NULL;
```

This way, your variables are safe for processing or to put into a DB without fear of SQL insertion attacks or what.

With regards your problem, there are several reasons why a session won't work but let's address the most obvious. In this case, your other page does not have session_start() at the top of it. In order to use sessions, you have to have this at the top of every page.

Question 43: Protecting image files and content with PHP

I am developing a site that requires logged in users to access the site. I have a custom authorization system that I have developed using php that works great. My problem is trying to protect non php content, specifically images. If someone knows the url of an image it can be linked to and anybody can view it, regardless as to whether they are logged in or not.

My solution must involve php protecting these files and not Apache. I do not know the passwords that my users use because they are stored in my database encrypted, so adding each user to the .htaccess file isn't an option.

One idea I had was to keep all my images in a directory outside of the web server root. Then when needing to display the image, I could open it up within php and then copy it to a directory that is accessible via the web. I could then setup a cron job that triggers a script that looks at all images in the public directory whose timestamp is older than a few seconds deleting any images from permanently being accessible from the web. My only concern is all of the work involved with doing this; awfully expensive method that could become a problem as the site gets larger and more people register.

Does anybody know of any good ways to protect these files using PHP?

A: A good way could be uploading them as binary data directly into your database.

In mysql, you can store them in a longblob column or a butea in postgreSQL.

You can also place them outside the webroot, but you don't need to move them. Just make a php script you use as an image in the image tag.

```
<img src="getuserimage.php?img=imgname.jpg" />
```

getuserimage.php could look like this;

```php
<?php
//check for right user-access before my code in this
script:

$imagedir = "../images_outside_webroot/";
$imgagename = stripslashes($_GET['imgname']);
$image = $imagedir.$imagename;
echo fread(fopen($image, "rb"), filesize($image));

?>
```

Question 44: Stop the caching of images in php session

Setting up a client editor (clients log in, session started) includes a preview page which shows current photos and a form for uploading photos to replace existing ones. Form is posted to a processing page which modifies and saves the image.
Client then returns to the preview page but old photos are still loading. I have tried setting various headers such as:

header("Cache-Control: post-check=0, pre-check=0", false);
header("Pragma: no-cache");
header("Expires: Mon, 26 Jul 1997 05:00:00 GMT");
header("Cache-Control: no-cache, no-store, must-revalidate");

I also tried using;
```
<meta http-equiv="Expires" content="Mon, 26 Jul 1997
05:00:00 GMT">
<META HTTP-EQUIV="CACHE-CONTROL" CONTENT="NO-CACHE">
```

and also tried using JavaScript to reload page:
```
window.location.reload(true);
```
But as it's a dynamic page, it just loops. How can I force the new updated pics to load automatically? How do I stop the caching of images in php session?

A: These headers only work with CSS, JavaScript, and HTML but doesn't work with images files like jpg and gif.

```
header("Expires: Mon, 26 Jul 1997 05:00:00 GMT");
header("Last-Modified: " . gmdate("D, d M Y H:i:s") .
" GMT");
header("Cache-Control: no-store, no-cache, must-
revalidate");
header("Cache-Control: post-check=0, pre-check=0",
false);
header("Pragma: no-cache");
```

To stop cache images, you can use this trick:
```
$var = md5(time());
$picture_name = "picture.jpg?var=".$var;
```

picture.jpg is the name of the file that you don't want cache.

Question 45: PHP - the right language

I'm looking to develop a highly scalable, high performance application (primarily search based) and would like to hear thoughts on whether PHP would be a good choice or should I stick with .Net or Java? What high trafficked sites are using PHP? In addition, are there any very solid frameworks you'd recommend (MVC, templating, etc.)?

A: Technically, all languages scale but some scale better than others.

PHP is made deliberately for serving web pages and focuses on that task. If your application is not web driven, I suggest another language such as Java or C.

As with all languages, PHP can do a lot but scalability of your applications depends on a lot of factors.

1. The scalability of your database.
2. The scalability of your OS.
3. The scalability of your hardware.
4. The scalability of your language.

This is why the LAMP stack (Linux, Apache, MySQL and PHP) is so popular because all aspects of the stack scale well.

Now used correctly with an MVC framework and only serving dynamic web pages, PHP can scale as well as everything else and can be very competitive beating even JAVA in several benchmarks. However, the more you have PHP doing aside from generating web pages, the more work your web server has to do and the more it gets bogged down.

Things such as dynamic image generation can be moved to Image Magick and handled on a separate server rather than using GD and trying to do it in PHP. So in other words, PHP can scale very well if you are smart about not having your web server handle more than it needs to and building your application to scale.

The application is only as good as the developer building it.

Question 46: Arrays not working

From mysql, I'm assigning the values to an array and printing out to check if the values are there. Then I read the array but the values have gone, except for the last value.

Here's the script followed by the output:

```
$start_date = array();

$query = "select * from NB_Reward_Data order by
start_date desc";
$result = mysql_query($query);
$num_results = mysql_num_rows($result);

for ($i=0; $i<$num_results; $i++)
{
echo "<BR /><BR />i = ".$i."<BR />";
$row = mysql_fetch_array($result);
$start_date = array($i=>$row['start_date']);
echo "start_date-array = ".$start_date[$i]."<BR /><BR
/>";
}

for ($i=0; $i<$num_results; $i++)
{
echo "<BR /><BR />i = ".$i."<BR />";
echo "start_date-array = ".$start_date[$i]."<BR /><BR
/>";
}
-----------------

Output:

i = 0
start_date-array = 2005-09-01

i = 1
start_date-array = 2005-09-01

i = 2
start_date-array = 2005-09-01

i = 3
start_date-array = 2004-01-01
```

```
i = 4
start_date-array = 2004-01-01

i = 5
start_date-array = 2004-01-01


i = 0
start_date-array =

i = 1
start_date-array =

i = 2
start_date-array =

i = 3
start_date-array =

i = 4
start_date-array =

i = 5
start_date-array = 2004-01-01
```

How can I make this work?

A: Check your code:

`$start_date = array($i=>$row['start_date']);` this line you used will overwrite any existing data in $start_date with new single item array so you get only last item in your output.

To add value of $row['start_date'] as new item to your existing array use:

`$start_date[] = $row['start_date'];`

Or to add it to specific array index use:
`$start_date[$i] = $row['start_date'];`

Question 47: File iteration and array values

I am iterating through a directory structure and would want to build an array in the process.

Here is what I did:

```php
<?php

$i=0;
$arr= array();
$fileArr = array();

$dh = opendir(".");

while ( $filename = readdir($dh) ) {
echo $filename."<br/>";
if (file_exists($filename)){
$content=file_get_contents($filename);
// do some parsing and the n put values in the
array..
$arr[i]["abc"] ="some value"+"$i";
$fileArr[i]["filename"] = $filename;
}
$i++;
}// end of while


print_r($arr);

print_r($fileArr);
?>
```

It is only showing the last one. The output is as follows:

Array ([i] => Array ([abc] => 19)) Array ([i] => Array ([filename] => cadence.csv))

What am I doing wrong?

A: You wrote only "i", that's JavaScript/Java style. Variables in PHP always begin with a "$".

You have an array element named "I" now because of the following:

1. PHP sees the "i" and thinks it is a constant.
2. PHP notices that i isn't a constant and now thinks that it is a string.
With error_reporting set to E_ALL you would get a parse error saying something like "unencapsed string" or so. I never read the exact error message; I just read file and line.

Question 48: Virtual server creation

Suppose I have uploaded a folder on my server, e.g.: http://www.mydomaindemo.com and the folder name is myfolder.

To view the content of folder through 'http' is: http:www.mydomaindemo.com/myfolder/.

How can I change existing url (existing url is: http:www.mydomaindemo.com/myfolder/) to http:myfolder.mydomaindemo.com?

A: Add this code into the httpd.conf file and then make the necessary changes to suit your requirements.

```
<VirtualHost 127.0.0.1>
ServerName myfolder.mydomaindemo.com
DocumentRoot "/www/webroot/dev"

<Directory "/www/webroot/dev">
order deny,allow
deny from all
allow from 127.0.0.1
</Directory>
</VirtualHost>
```

One more example:

```
<VirtualHost 127.0.0.1>
ServerAdmin admin@wwwdomain.com
DocumentRoot var/www/html/www
ServerName www.domain.com
ErrorLog /var/log/httpd/www_domain_e.log
CustomLogi /var/log/httpd/www_domain_a.log common
</VirtualHost>
```

```
<VirtualHost 127.0.0.1>
ServerAdmin admin@sub1domain.com
DocumentRoot /var/www/html/sub1
ServerName sub1.domain.com
ErrorLog /var/log/httpd/sub1_domain_e.log
CustomLog /var/log/httpd/sub1_domain_a.log common
```

```
</VirtualHost>

<VirtualHost 127.0.0.1>
ServerAdmin admin@sub2domain.com
DocumentRoot /var/www/html/sub2
ServerName sub2.domain.com
ErrorLog /var/log/httpd/sub2_domain_e.log
CustomLog /var/log/httpd/sub2_domain_a.log common
</VirtualHost>
```

Question 49: Multiple action form

I have a form in which there are 2 buttons, depending on which button user will click, form should be linked by submission to different pages. Example:

```
Button = "Submit" -> confirm.php
Button = "Go Back" -> create.php
```

I know that form can have only one action, but somehow I need to manipulate this probably using Javascript? Is there a way to do this?

A: Make use of this:

```
<html>
<head>
<script language='javascript'>
function move(choice)
{
if(choice == 1)
page='create.php'
else
page='confirm.php'

document.getElementById('formName').action = page;
document.getElementById('formName').submit();
}

</script>
</head>

<body>
<form name="formName" id="formName" method="post">
<input type="button" name="backBut" id="backBut"
value="Go Back" onclick="javascript:move('1');">
<input type="button" name="confirmBut"
id="confirmBut" value="Confirm"
onclick="javascript:move('2');">
</form>
</body>
</html>
```

Question 50: Develop PHP

I want to be able to code PHP and SQL using IIS server. I have Dreamweaver MX, XP professional and MySQL. Can I do it with this environment or do I need any other software? Do I also need Apache?

A: You can develop PHP applications without apache, but these would run from a command line (e.g. DOS command line).

The most common way however is for PHP to be generating HTML pages dynamically. In that case you need to install the Apache web server (so that you can actually have your PHP files processing and creating HTML pages on the fly). It sounds pretty scary, but it's not fancier than having any other program running and shouldn't be much trickier to get running either. Go for Apache 1.x rather than Apache 2.x, this is the most stable/reliable version.

Question 51: PHP vs. PERL

What are the differences and advantages between PHP and PERL?

A: Perl is powerful, yet outdated, scripting language better suited for systems administration, Linux scripts, and file processing.

PHP is powerful, easy to learn yet hard to master, scripting language specifically suited for web design.

PHP and PERL are systems that can be used for web design or systems administration but each has its own specialty.

PHP or Ruby on rails is best suited for design: http://www.rubyonrails.com is best suited for the novice as it handles many of the mundane stuff for you.

Question 52: PHP vs. ASP.NET

When it comes to web development these days you have a lot of options. Which of these two (PHP or ASP.NET) would you use to develop a strong, professional and secure web application?

A: In terms of features, you can do pretty much the same things in either language. PHP is free, open source, with tons of tutorials and resources out there. Not to mention it works with both Windows and UNIX.

Question 53: Spaces between words

I wrote a page to have 3 drop-downs based on car year, make and model data in a MySQL database. The 3 drop-downs are dependent on one another. The problem is with the second drop-down selection. The logic works fine if the selected value is a single word but doesn't work if there is a space in between any of the words.

Example: Year selected is 1981. Make selected is Audi. The third drop-down shows all the models for 1981 Audi's.

Example showing the problem: Year selected is 1981. Make selected is American Motors. The third drop-down fails because the value passed from the second drop-down is "American" and not "American Motors". So the third drop-down is bombing because it's not finding a corresponding model for "American". I know the value is correct coming from the database because I see "American Motors" as a selection in the second drop-down but the "Motors" part is being lost somewhere from the click to when it is read by the submit.

Here's my code for the second drop-down. I have done all the drop-downs in the same way. I can tell by testing that the "Motors" part is not there by the time it gets to the sql statement for the final drop-down.

```
echo "<p align='left'>Vehicle Make:   ";
if ($_POST['VehicleYear'] != "")
 {
  $query='SELECT distinct vehiclemake FROM
vehicledata WHERE vehicleyear =
'.$_POST['VehicleYear'];
  $result=mysql_query($query);
  $num_results = mysql_num_rows($result) or die ("num
result failed ln 55");
  echo '<select name="VehicleMake"
onchange="this.form.submit()">';
  echo '<option value="Select Make" selected>Select
Make</option>';
  $vehyeari = $_POST['VehicleYear'];
  $vehmake = isset($_POST["VehicleMake"]) ?
$_POST["VehicleMake"] : "";
  if ($vehmakei == "")
```

```
    {
     $makeselected = "Select Make";
    }
     else
    {
     $makeselected = $vehmake;
    }
    for ($i=0; $i < $num_results; $i++)
   {
    $row = mysql_fetch_array($result);
    $make = stripslashes($row['vehiclemake']);
     if ($make == $makeselected)
     {
     echo "<option value=$make
selected>$make</option><br>";
     }
     else
     {
     echo "<option value=$make>$make</option><br>";
     }
}
 echo "</select><br><br><br>";
} //end of main if on make section
 echo "</p>";
```

What is wrong with my code?

A: You need to enclose the value in quotes:

CODE:
```
   echo "<option value=\"$make\"
selected>$make</option><br>";
     }
     else
     {
     echo "<option
value=\"$make\">$make</option><br>";
```

Question 54: Mail subject confusion

I want to perform a simple mail function and have to send the recipient 4 text boxes and one drop down list selection.

My problem lies in the fact that when I test this email, the subject is fine (as it is hardcoded), however the sender says it is from "CGI-Mailer" with a reply to address of the host server (where ever that may be).

My code looks like this:

HTML form

CODE:
```
<form action="send.php" method="post">
    <p>Name</p>
        <p><input type="text" name="name"
maxlength="40"></p>
    <p>Phone</p>
        <p><input type="text" name="phone"
maxlength="14"></p>
    <p>Email</p>
        <p><input type="text" name="email"
maxlength="40"></p>
    <p>Type of site</p>
    <p><select name="type">
        <option value="No option selected">Please
select an option...</option>
        <option value="Option one">Option 1</option>
        <option value="Option two">Option 2</option>
        <option value="Option three">Option
3</option>
        <option value="option 4 :D">option 4</option>
        <option value="option five">option 5</option>
    </select></p>
    <p>Additional Information</p>
        <textarea name="comments" rows="10"
cols="40"></textarea>
    <input name="submit" type="submit" value="send">
</form>
```

My PHP looks like this:

CODE:

```php
<?php
@extract($_POST);
//$from = "From: $name < $email >";
$sentby = "Quote / Enquiry requested by:\n$name <
$email >\nPhonei number: $phone\n\nType of site:
$type";
mail('dan@mysite.co.uk','Website
Enquiry',$comments,$sentby);
?>
```

When I receive a mail, the format is like this:
Subject reads "Website Enquiry" and the sender is "CGI-Mailer"

Everything else is formatted correct. I have tried moving parts around but if I change the order of the To, Subject and Message, the whole layout of the received email goes wrong.

What is the possible cause of this problem?

A: The one possible cause of the problem is that you are not setting a "From:" header.

The PHP online manual entry for mail() (http://us3.php.net/manual/en/function.mail.php) also mentions that you should separate headers with CRLF (\r\n).

Note: When sending mail, the mail must contain a "From" header. This can be set with the additional_headers parameter or a default can be set in php.ini.

In your case, a default sender was set in your php.ini: CGI-Mailer. Your code now overrides the default.

Question 55: Parse error & unexpected character in phpinfo

I'm trying to run php4 CGI script that only contains:

CODE:
```php
<?php
phpinfo();
?>
```
It runs fine when I call it from terminal or command line. There are no errors. However, when I call it from the browser I get the following error:
Quote:
```
Warning: Unexpected character in input: " (ASCII=19)
state=1 in /usr/bin/php4-cgi on line 2353

Parse error: parse error, unexpected '*' in
/usr/bin/php4-cgi on line 2353
```

Apache info that may be relevant:
CODE:
```
AddHandler php-script .php
ScriptAlias /cgi-bin/ /usr/bin/
Action php-script /cgi-bin/php4-cgi
```

Why am I getting this error?

A: The reason it works fine from the command line is you're just running the PHP interpreter and your issue seems to be in the php4-cgi handler.

The first thing I'd say is to consider running it as an Apache module instead. It's significantly faster and you won't run into these issues.

The second thing is, this is a problem with the php4 install... did you compile it, is it a package (if so where'd you get it), and what's your OS? A re-install is your easiest fix, but your best route depends on those details. If you're running something like Debian, you may have just snagged a bad package. In my experience very few people run php as a cgi anymore, so it's not surprising something like that could slip through.

Question 56: Strip Letters from Variable

I have variables pulled from a db which are similar to:
SA1
SA2
SA3

I am trying to remove the SA from the variable so I'm just left with 1, 2, and 3.

I had a look at trim and split but unable to find a relevant example.

What is the correct method to go about it?

A: Try str_replace() (replace "SA" with an empty string).

Question 57: Get column names and data

I'm trying to get all the column names in a row and then get the data for each row. I can do both of these separately. These are all in MySQL database.

The problem I am having is that I need to check whether or not the column has data in it for that row. If there's none, I need not include it into the output variable.

What is the best way to do this?

A: A mysql_fetch_assoc() fetches data from a MySQL results in a handle getting into an associative array. There are column names and values all at once.

If you want to get all the column names first, issue a DESCRIBE tablename query and fetch the results of that query. This will give all the information you will ever need about your table, and you can follow that query with a SELECT query.

Question 58: MySQL to XML in PHP

I would like to convert a MySQL database to xml. I want to display a table of customer details for members to download. How can I do this?

A: An XML is just a structured text (albeit in a strict format). Just use php to select the records and fields you want, iterate through the record set and dump out text to a file in the same way that you would dump text to a browser remembering, of course, to put the right tags around each record and field.

Let's assume your table for users is:
id first_name last_name user_id

Write something like this:
CODE:

```
<?
$xmlfile = "";//file name
$fh = fopen ($xmlfile ,"wb") or die ("cant create
file");

$sql = "Select id, first_name, last_name, user_id
from usertable";

$result = @mysql_query($sql) or die (mysql_error());
while ($row[] = mysql_fetch_assoc($result)):
//do nothing
endwhile;
$lineterminate = chr(13) .chr(10);

fwrite ($fh, "<?xml
version="1.0"?>$lineterminate<users>");
foreach ($row as $val):
extract($val);
$line = "
<user> $lineterminatei
<id> $lineterminate
$id $lineterminate
</id> $lineterminate
<first_name> $lineterminate
$first_name $lineterminate
</first_name> $lineterminate
<last_name> $lineterminate
```

```
$last_name $lineterminate
</last_name> $lineterminate
</user> $lineterminate
";
fwrite($fh, $line);
endforeach;
fwrite ($fh, "</users>");
?>
```

Question 59: if/else

What is this called?

```
true?doA():doB();
```

Is it the equivalent of?

```
if (true){ doA; }
else {do B; }
```

I just want to make sure that the FIRST statement is executed if true, the SECOND if false. Is this right?

A: Yes, it is. And you're right, it's equivalent. It's shorthand for the if-then-else statements.

```
$x = $a == 5 ? true : notfive();
```

```
$x will be true if $a == 5, or the return value from
function notfive() otherwise.
```

See the section titled "Ternary Operator" here:
http://www.php.net/operators.comparison

Question 60: PHP, MS SQL, ntext field problem

The error I get is:
Unicode data in a Unicode-only collation or ntext data cannot be sent to clients using DB-Library (such as ISQL) or ODBC version 3.7 or earlier.

This error occurs when running any SELECT query that attempts to pull an ntext field. I am using the mssql functions in PHP to do so. What is causing this problem?

A: This is a problem with odbc.

Workaround: Cast the field as a text field in your query.

Example: select cast(field2 as text) as field2 from table.

Question 61: Redirect

This is a simple unsecured username and password procedure I am using. The redirect works for the first if, but the next if statement does not work.

CODE:
```
<html>
<head>
<title>Displaying the Inputted Information</title>
</head>

<body>
<?php

// obtaining the information from the form and
displaying it,

if (($txt_username == building9) && ($txt_password ==
li))
{

('Location: http://www.meadowbrokpoi.com/purchaser-
bld.htm');
exit();

}
elseif (($txt_username != building9) &&
($txt_password != li))
{

header('Location: http://www.failure.com);
exit();

}


elseif (($txt_username == building8) &&
($txt_password == fn))
{

('Location: http://www.meado.com/purchaser-
bug8.htm');
exit();

}
```

```
else (($txt_username != building8) && ($txt_password
!= fn))
{

header('Location: http://www.failure.com);
exit();

}

?>

</body>
</html>
```

Can I only have one redirect in this code?

A: When we're at headers, you can have as many as you want in different blocks in your code. As long as you know that as soon as your code hits one, it will redirect to the next page and stop executing the code on the current.

Headers are something that is sent before the output is started. That means that all the header calls must be made before any output is made to the browser. This includes:

a) Any html code outside php tags (this is what you have);
b) Any whitespace or carriage returns before php tags (this is what you could also have);
c) Any print or echo statement;
d) Any error that outputs to the browser.

Make sure you don't have any of that before the header call and you'll be ok.

Question 62: PHP Upload - Allow .exe files

This page is going to be in a protected area that I will be using to upload basic programs that I need when I am out at customers sites, once uploaded I will store their link in a mysql db and post it on a html page.

Currently, I am using the following to test an upload page I am building.
CODE:

```
<form enctype="multipart/form-data" action="test.php"
method="post">
  <div align="center">
    <p>
      Upload</p>
    <p><input name="userfile" type="file" /><br />
      <input type="submit" value="Upload" />
    </p>
  </div>
</form>

<?php
$uploaddir = '/var/www/website/uploaddir/';
$uploadfile = $uploaddir .
$_FILES['userfile']['name'];

print "<pre>";
if
(move_uploaded_file($_FILES['userfile']['tmp_name'],
$uploadfile)) {
    echo "The file ". basename(
$_FILES['userfile']['name']). " has been uploaded";
} else{
    echo "There was an error uploading the file,
please try again!";
}
?>
```

I can successfully upload .zip, jpg etc files, but haven't been able to allow .exe files. Do I need to add something to allow .exe uploads?

A: To the best of my knowledge, there is no limit in PHP to the type of file that can be uploaded to a script.

There may be, however, limits imposed by the size of a file, the amount of time a script can run, or other limits imposed by your web server.

Question 63: Empty a file

I open a file and read in some values and then feed the file into another function. I want to empty the file again for the next time.

There doesn't seem to be much functionality to fwrite(), it doesn't give me the option of writing over the previous file contents.
CODE:

```
$filename = './templates/Classic/pad.tpl';
 $fp = fopen($filename, "a");
 flock($fp, LOCK_EX);
 $string = $output;
 if ( !fputs($fp, $string) ) { die("There was an
error writing to the file 1"); }
 $template->set_filenames( array('fckeditor' =>
'./templates/Classic/pad.tpl') );
 if ( !fwrite($fp, ' ') ) { die("There was an error
writing to the file 2"); }

 flock($fp, LOCK_UN);
 fclose($fp);
```

Is there any way to empty a file in php?

A: It all depends on what mode you use in fopen().

In the code above, you are using 'a' which is used when you want to append the file contents. You will probably want to use 'w' or 'w+'. Both of these place the file pointer at the beginning of the file and truncate the file length to zero (erase the contents, in a sense). The 'w+' is used when you want to read and write to the file. A 'w' is used when you only want to write to the file.

Question 64: SQL -> CSV (with commas in data)

I am doing a database extract to CSV for member addresses and can"t figure out how to escape the ,'s that exist in my data so that they won't act as column separators. I have tried back slashing them dynamically, but that doesn't help.

How can I overcome this problem?

A: Have the fields separated by quotes as well as commas. Most CSV parsers should be savvy enough to understand that anything in the quotes is part of the field (as long as they don't contain quotes as well!) and will thus ignore any commas inside of quotes. Otherwise it depends on the final output of the data in the CSV file. For example; if it's going to html you can change all the commas to , before making it a CSV file. I've mostly been using PERL to handle CSV files, but PHP should work as well.

Question 65: Arrays

I have two pages, one displaying a form from a database which allows a user to change the status of a job via a drop down box, see Page1.php code below
Page1.php

CODE:
```
    while($row = mysql_fetch_array($result))
    {
        echo "<tr align='center'>\n";
        extract($row);
        echo '<td>
                <select name="AwaitingStatus[]"
class="body">
                <option value="">Change
Status...</option>
                <option value="P">Awaiting Spare
Parts</option>
                <option value="U">Awaiting
Tools/Equipment</option>
                <option value="K">Awaiting Mod
Kits</option>
                <option value="I">Awaiting
Inspection</option>
                <option value="V">Awaiting Tech.
Services</option>
                <option value="B">Awaiting
Access</option>
                <option value="Q">Awaiting Other
Staff/Jobs</option>
                <option value="F">Change of
Priority</option>
                <option value="E">Card
Completion</option>
                <option value="X">System
Fault</option>
                <option value="Z">Awaiting
Planning</option>
            </select></td>';
        echo "<td>".$row['jobTitle']."</td>\n";
        echo "<input type='hidden' name='hidvar[]'
value='$jobCode'";
        echo "</tr>\n";
    }
```

This code now posts the variables to Page2.php and processes it
i.e.
Page2.php
CODE:

```
    foreach ($AwaitingStatus as $JobStatus)
//Checks for Status Change
    {
        foreach ($jobCode as $Code)
        {
            $sql3 = "UPDATE joblist SET LostTime =
'$JobStatus' WHERE jobCode = '$Code'";
            $Code = mysql_query($sql3);
            echo $sql3.'<br>';
        }
        echo "<br />";
    }
```

The problem with this code is that it outputs;

CODE:

```
UPDATE joblist SET LostTime = 'U' WHERE jobCode =
'CG162'
UPDATE joblist SET LostTime = 'U' WHERE jobCode =
'RS976'

UPDATE joblist SET LostTime = 'I' WHERE jobCode =
'CG162'
UPDATE joblist SET LostTime = 'I' WHERE jobCode =
'RS976'
```

Whereas, I just want it to update;

CODE:

```
UPDATE joblist SET LostTime = 'I' WHERE jobCode =
'RS976'
UPDATE joblist SET LostTime = 'U' WHERE jobCode =
'CG162'
```

If I output the array structure and values;
CODE:

```
    print_r ($AwaitingStatus);
    print_r ($jobCode);
```

It returns;

CODE:
```
Array ( [0] => U [1] => I ) Array ( [0] => CG162 [1]
=> RS976 )
```

I'm sure the problem is within the foreach loop.

CODE:
```
foreach ($AwaitingStatus as $JobStatus)
{
    foreach ($jobCode as $Code)
    {
    }
}
```

How can I achieve this without it looping again?

A: You could use a 'for' loop instead of a foreach:

CODE:
```
$count = count($AwaitingStatus);
for($i=0; $i<$count; $i++)
{
    //check that 'status' has some value
    if (!empty($AwaitingStatus[$i])) {
        $sql3 = "UPDATE joblist
                SET LostTime = '$AwaitingStatus[$i]'
                WHERE jobCode = '$jobCode[$i]'";

        $Code = mysql_query($sql3);
        echo $sql3.'<br /><br />';
    }
}
```

You may want to look at empty() in the PHP Manual to see what PHP considers empty.

Question 66: Automating tasks at set intervals

I am in the process of developing a script to upload images to a web server (via FTP) from a PC running one or more web cams. FTP sides of things are sorted.

I'm now trying to work out the best angle to approach automating the uploading of images at a set interval.

My intended routes so far are:

1) Set cron job to run every minute of the day.
2) PHP script will only execute image uploads between hours of 8am and 6pm.
3) PHP Script will upload images every 5 seconds.

My idea is to use some sort of while loop (after adjusting maximum script execution time to 60 seconds) which would check to see if the second at execution was one of the following;

CODE:
```
00, 05, 10, 15, 20, 25, 30 ...
```

If the second at execution matched one of the above then it would perform an upload, if not then it wouldn't.

Could someone advise me on the most appropriate REGEX string which return true if a match was found?

A: Simply do this code:

```
if (time()%5 == 0)
```

Question 67: Value from database to form only displays firstword

I have a form that when the value is called from database, it will only display the first word in the text input field. If I change it to a text area or when it is called anywhere else on the site, it displays correctly.

What is causing this problem?

A: There are a couple of possible problems:

1. You are not quoting the value in the text box.

CODE:
```
<input type="text" name="text box"
value="<?=$row['fieldname']?>" />
```
without the quotes, the value will stop after the first space.

2. Your db values contain carriage returns. If so, strip them out first.

Question 68: Find out if insert is successful or not

I'm writing a script which will upload a CSV file and insert the records into a mysql database. I want the user to act on any unsuccessful inserts. Is there any way if I can find out for each insert whether or not the insert statement was successful?

A: From http://us2.php.net/manual/en/function.mysql-query.php:

"For other type of SQL statements, UPDATE, DELETE, DROP, etc, mysql_query() returns TRUE on success or FALSE on error."

Try evaluating the return from mysql_query().

Question 69: Present flash in PHP script

I have the following code:

```
<?
if(!empty($_SESSION[MemberID]))
{
    $LoginLogout = "<a href=\"logout.php\"><embed
SRC=\"images/logout.swf\" WIDTH=100 HEIGHT=50
ALT=\"Login\" border=0></embed></a>";

    if(ereg("index.php", $_SERVER[SCRIPT_NAME]))
    {
        $WelcomeMessage =
nl2br($aset[message])."<br><hr width=\"100%\" size=1
color=dddddd>";
    }
}
else
{
    $LoginLogout = "<a href=\"login.php\"><img
SRC=\"images/login.swf\" WIDTH=100 HEIGHT=50
ALT=\"Login\" border=0></a>";

}
?>
```

Instead of images, I have a flash file that I want to use but it will not bring up anything. Where am I going wrong?

A: Let's dissect your string $LoginLogout:

CODE:
```
$LoginLogout = "<object width="550" height="400">
<param name="movie" value="images/logout.swf">
<embed src="images/logout.swf" width="550"
height="400">
</embed>
</object>";
```

Your string starts "<object width= then PHP finds a closing double quote ", it thinks the string has ended. However, a little

down the line it finds another "and" there it should have given you an error.

You have to learn how to use the quotes for strings in PHP; it is either double quotes surrounding single ones or single quotes surrounding double quotes. So if your string starts with double quotes every quote inside is should have to be a single quote.

Try the following:

CODE:
```
$LoginLogout = "<object width='550' height='400'>
<param name='movie' value='images/logout.swf'>
<embed src='images/logout.swf' width='550'
height='400'>
</embed>
</object>";
```

Question 70: Information from MS SQL Stored Procedure

I can run a query directly from the database.

CODE:
```
$db = mssql_connect("server","user","password") or
die("Unable to connect to server");
$db = mssql_select_db("database");

$query = mssql_init("ProcedureName",$db);
$result = mssql_execute($query) or die("QUERY
FAILED");

print("<table border=1>");
print("<tr><th>Header 1</th><th>Header 2</th></tr>");
while ($row = mssql_fetch_object($result)) {
print("<tr>");
printf("<td>%s</td>", $row->FirstName);
printf("<td>%s</td>", $row->LastName);
print("</tr>");
}
print("</table>");
```

How can I successfully get information from a stored procedure in MS SQL?

A: You are assigning $db to the database connection. To open database, remove $db = from the select db line and you'll be good to go.

Question 71: Get URL of whole page thru script in an include

My site uses Includes for header, main menu, etc. I use the require("include.htm") method. I want to have a script in one of the Includes which can read the URL of the final composite page.

I have a lot of technical content on many individual pages people like to link to. I want to generate a ready made copy and paste text box on each page so they can paste the link into their website.

I would like "<a href="abc.php" target="blank">, this page is about abc</a>" to appear in part of the included page's area.

I want to do this in PHP, not Javascript.

How do I add a script to every page and do it through a single include page?

A: You should take a look at the documentation for the $_SERVER superglobal:

http://us3.php.net/reserved.variables;

Something like $_SERVER["REQUEST_URI"] will do the trick.

Question 72: Use PHP Includes other than for ease of editing

Why would I want to use PHP Includes other than making it easy to edit one code that is used across the entire site? Does it FOR SURE make the page load quicker?

A: Most performance issues are rooted in inefficient coding or underpowered hardware. Including shared libraries using include() with file system access is very quick and should not pose any significant performance loss. Overall the maintenance of clean code, the use of classes, external modules, PEARL, etc. leaves no other choice as to include code from other files.

The only thing to discourage is to include files using wrappers that e.g. fetch the content via http. As long as you use file system based includes you should be absolutely safe. The minor (probably not noticeable) "loss" of performance is outweighed by the advantages of the organization of a code base. Look at it as a given; there is no other sensible way of coding.

Question 73: Day of week from Date

If I have a date (e.g. "25/03/2005" (UK format)), how do I find what day of the week this date relates to?

A: Use
```
$tmp = explode("/", '21/11/2005');
print date("l", mktime(0,0,0,$tmp[1], $tmp[0], $tmp[2]));
```

Question 74: Kill Session

What is the best method to kill a session completely?

A: Do this:

CODE:
```
session_destroy()
```

Or this:
CODE:
```
$_SESSION = array();
if (isset($_COOKIE[session_name()]))
setcookie(session_name(), '', time()-42000, '/');
session_destroy();
```

Question 75: Directory with 0777 access

In order to allow my visitors to upload .jpg pictures to my site, I have created a directory with access rights set to 0777. This is the only setting that I got working.

Now this directory is a target for hackers. They managed to create a directory under that directory and put stuff there with malicious intent. How can I prevent this?

Do I have to change the access right in the upload script?

A: Create the upload directory from within PHP, this way it will be owned and read only by your webserver (apache), this removes the need for it to be 0777 (it should end up as 755 or less).

Simply make sure that the user on which Apache runs is the owner of the directory and make sure that user has permission to write.

Question 76: Security with db connection

I include a separate PHP page on each of my website's pages that contains mysql_connect and mysql_select_db. Is there any security risk with this? Or since PHP is processed on the server end it doesn't matter?

A: I strongly recommend that the included file reside on the file system outside of the document root of your web site. That way, if something should happen to your web server's configuration that would allow PHP files to be sent to a browser as-is (send them, rather than running them and sending the output), your password will not be exposed.

I also recommend that you lock down the privileges of the login user of your script as much as possible. MySQL, for example, gives the ability to allow a user to login only from certain IP locations. If your script's MySQL user could only login from localhost (assuming that your web server is also your database server), then the value of that login is reduced to a hostile entity.

PHP's include(), include_once(), require() and require_once() functions are not constrained by the current document_root. You can put the files anywhere on the filesystem and still include them. You just have to specify the correct path.

Question 77: Multiple Submit

I want to know if a category hasn't been selected not to do an INPUT for a particular course ID. Right now, for however many courses are listed on the page, it submits all into the database even if I didn't pick a category for it. I need only the courses where I select a category from the dropdown to be submitted.

Here's my code:

```
$editFormAction = $_SERVER['PHP_SELF'];
if (isset($_SERVER['QUERY_STRING'])) {
$editFormAction .= "?" .
htmlentities($_SERVER['QUERY_STRING']);
}

if ((isset($_POST["MM_insert"])) &&
($_POST["MM_insert"] == "category"))

$count = count ($_POST['catid']);

for ($i=0; $i < $count; $i++) {

$corid = $_POST['corid'][$i];
$catid = $_POST['catid'][$i];

mysql_query ("INSERT INTO spec_coursecats (catid,
corid)
VALUES ('$catid', '$corid')");

}
```

And the code that creates my dropdown for Categories;

```
function addOptions($parent,$depth) {
$sql = $parent>0 ? "select catid,catname from
spec_categories where subcatid = $parent ORDER BY
catname ASC"
: "select catid,catname from spec_categories where
subcatid is null ORDER BY catname ASC" ;
$res = mysql_query($sql);
$indent =
str_repeat('     ',$depth);
// indent subcats according to depth of call
while (list($id, $desc) = mysql_fetch_row($res)) {
echo "<option value=\"$id\">$indent$desc</option>";
```

```
/* the recursive bit */
addOptions($id, $depth+1); // add options for those
whose parent is this id
}
```

And my Form code;

```
<form action="<?php echo $editFormAction; ?>"
method="POST" name="category" id="category">
        <table width="938" border="0" cellpadding="0"
cellspacing="0" class="font">
            <?php do { ?>
            <tr>
                <td width="29"><a
href="courseedit.php?recordID=<?php echo
$row_rs_course['corid']; ?>"
class="font">Edit</a> </td>
                <td><?php echo
$row_rs_course['course_num']; ?> - <?php echo
$row_rs_course['ctitle']; ?> </td>
                <td align="right">


<select name="catid[]" id="catid[]">
<option value="" selected>Select one</option>
<?php
addOptions(0,0); // call to recursive function
?></select>

                    <input name="corid[]" type="hidden"
id="corid[]" value="<?php echo
$row_rs_course['corid']; ?>">               </td>
                <td width="55" align="right"><a
href="../dbs/admindelete.php?corid=<?php echo
$row_rs_course['corid']; ?>" class="delete">
  Delete   </a> </td>
            </tr>
            <?php } while ($row_rs_course =
mysql_fetch_assoc($rs_course)); ?>
        <tr>
            <td> </td>
            <td> </td>
            <td colspan="2" align="left"><input
name="categoryset" type="submit" id="categoryset"
value="Submit"> <input type="reset" name="Reset"
value="Reset">
            </td>
        </tr></table>
```

```
        <input type="hidden" name="MM_insert"
value="category">
    </form>
```

Is there a way to achieve this?

A: Yes. You do have to check for empties though:

```
if(!empty($_POST['corid'][$i]))
{
$corid = $_POST['corid'][$i];
$catid = $_POST['catid'][$i];
mysql_query ("INSERT INTO spec_coursecats (catid,
corid)
VALUES ('$catid', '$corid')");
}
```

Question 78: CSV File

Is there a way to create a CSV file using PHP and pulling the data from MySQL?

A: Yes, there is a way to do this. We currently do it from an MSSQL table, so a MySQL table shouldn't be much different.

First you want to make sure the proper header goes out:

CODE:
```
Header("Content-type: text");
Header("Content-Disposition: attachment;
filename=invoice.nonedi.zzprecdata");
```

Then as you are going through your records, just output them like you would to the screen.

CODE:
```
echo "$Field1,$Field2,$Filed3,$Fieldn\n";
```

And when your PHP finally finishes executing, your download is complete.

Question 79: Checking previous mysql results

I am writing a script that allows people to book multiple rental properties for corporate events. They enter the number of people that will attend the event and are given a selection of properties that match their needs for the group. A list of properties is presented and they can book.

The problem is on some of the results. For example, they may need accommodations for 12 people. The PHP script queries the database, and may come up with apartments that sleep the following: 4 people, 3 people, 4 people, 2 people. This gives 13 people and not a problem.

However, sometimes the choices are 4 people, 4 people, 3 people, and 4 people.
Obviously, this gives 15 people whereas if the 3 person apartment was not given, it would be the requisite 12.

Is there any easy way I can check the results of my query and avoid this kind of problem?

A: You can order on as many parameters as you want. The selection will be sorted on the first, within that on the second and so on. Just separate the parameters with comma after the ORDER BY. You can add 'DESC' next to any parameter if you want descending rather then ascending sorting.

Question 80: mktime bug

I want to put: "12-25-2004 0:0:0" on the screen.

But the following code:
```
echo date('d-m-Y H:m:s', mktime(0,0,0,12,25,1978));
```

Returns as:
```
25-Dec-1978 12:12:00
```

What is happening?

A: To create your results, I had to change your code to:

```
echo date('d-M-Y m:m:s', mktime(0,0,0,12,25,1978));
```

mktime() is working fine; check the syntax for the date() function.

Check this site:
http://us2.php.net/manual/en/function.date.php

Question 81: Regular expressions

I need to parse a string and replace newline characters (either '\n' or'\r') with <p> tags. Is preg_replace() the best function for this?

If there are two or more newline tags together, they must only produce one <p> tag. So if the string contained '\n\n\n' or '\r\r\r' or '\n\r', I'd need to replace it with a single <p>.

Is there an easy expression for this?

A: That regular expression is actually easier than you might think. Its English translation would be, "Any number of newlines or carriage returns in a row".

This script:

```php
<?php

$a = array ("\r", "\n", "\r\n", "\r\r", "\n\n",
"\r\n\r\n", "\r\r\n", "a\ra", "a\r\na", "\ra\r",
"\r\na\r\n");

$a = preg_replace ("/([\r\n])+/", '<p>', $a);

print_r ($a);
?>
```

Outputs:
```
Array
(
    [0] => <p>
    [1] => <p>
    [2] => <p>
    [3] => <p>
    [4] => <p>
    [5] => <p>
    [6] => <p>
    [7] => a<p>a
    [8] => a<p>a
    [9] => <p>a<p>
    [10] => <p>a<p>
)
```

Question 82: Export to MS Excel Format

I created a script to search into my database to retrieve certain information that I need.

How can I export the result of the query to a MS Excel file?

A: Export to CSV is possibly the easiest format to get excel to read. Otherwise it's going to require (probably) both of these:

a) Bashing programming manuals on COM.
b) Having an M$ powered server with Excel installed.

I don't think there's actually any other way to do this without a) or b).

The following code is called from a form submitting the query to save.php, it's an old code, so the variables aren't set using $_POST or $_GET. You may need to change these. It basically dumps the data to a download stream offering the option to save or open (c/o your browser seeing what's coming).

`save.php`

CODE:
```
<?
//configure the database here, or pass it along with
$sql (the query) and $query (the value used to name
the file).
$db="database";

// I use a config.inc.php with the database
connection details, include one here if required
//require('config.inc.php');


if(!isset($sql)){
   echo "No Query";
   exit;
     }else{
     $sql=stripslashes($sql);
     $file=$query.".csv";
```

```
}

header("Content-Type: application/vnd.ms-excel");
header("Content-Disposition:
attachment;filename=".$file );
header('Pragma: no-cache');
header('Expires: 0');

mysql_select_db($db,$connection);
$result = mysql_query($sql,$connection);
if($result){


    $columns=@mysql_num_fields($result);
for ($i = 0; $i < mysql_num_fields($result); $i++) {

    print "\"".mysql_field_name($result,$i)."\",";

}
echo "\n";

while ($myrow = mysql_fetch_array($result)){
    for ($i = 0; $i < ($columns); $i++) {
        echo "\"".$myrow[$i]."\",";
    }
        echo "\n";
}
}else{
echo "No results";
}

?>
```

Another way is to just use HTML tags:

Sample CODE:
```
<table border="1">
<tr>
<td>column 1</td>
<td>column 2</td>
</tr>
</table>
```

This will create a table in excel using the table's TR as rows and TD as cells just like in html.

Question 83: Create an array with multiple entries per value

I have an array which is populated by codes that I use in various queries and functions. I want to include a second entry into the array so that I can also include a name.

I currently have:
```
Array = (ACC01,
         ACC02,
         ADV02)
```

I now want:
```
Array = (ACC01 Accord Inc,
         ACC02 Acctune Inc,
         ADV02 Advanced Inc)
```

I need the code and name separately as the code is submitted later on.
My option is to put in some character like 'ACC01|Accord Inc' and then script to remove the character to process. Is there a better and simpler way?

A: You need a multidimensional array. PHP tends to think of these kinds of things as arrays of arrays.

Something like:

```
CODE:
$foo = array
(
    array ('ACC01', 'Accord Inc.'),
    array ('ACC02', 'Acctune Inc'),
    array ('ADV02', 'Advanced Inc')
);
```

will give you a multidimensional array with numerical subscripts. $foo[0][0] would be 'ACC01' and $foo[1][1] would be 'Acctune Inc'.

You could also use associative arrays:

CODE:
```
$foo = array
(
    array ('code' => 'ACC01', 'name' => 'Accord
Inc.'),
    array ('code' => 'ACC02', 'name' => 'Acctune
Inc'),
    array ('code' => 'ADV02', 'name' => 'Advanced
Inc')
);
```

Thus $foo[0]['code'] would be 'ACC01' and
$foo[1]['name'] would be "Acctune Inc'.

You could also have an associative array like:

CODE:
```
$foo = array ('ACC01' => 'Accord Inc.',
              'ACC02' => 'Acctune Inc',
              'ADV02' => 'Advanced Inc')
);
```

Question 84: Loading file names into an Array

I need a rotating picture at the top of a webpage. I need to do this without a db (i.e. mysql). I am trying to modify some code I found.

CODE:
```
srand((float) microtime() * 10000000);
  $image[1]='/location/of/image1.jpg';
  $image[2]='/location/of/image2.jpg';
  $image[3]='/location/of/image3.jpg';
  $image[4]='/location/of/image4.jpg';
  $image[5]='/location/of/image5.jpg';
  $rn = array_rand($image);
echo '<img src="'.$image[$rn].'">';
```

I would like to count the number of files in a dir and load an array with the file names (ie $image[1]=$file_name_one_blah, $image[2]=$file_name_two_blah), pick a rand num, and display the random pic.

What do I need to do this?

A: This can perform what you need. It opens a dir and puts all the files into an array.

CODE:
```
$dir="somedirectory";
//check that $dir really exists
    if(is_dir($dir)){
//initialize counter
    $num_files="0";
//initialize files array
    $file_list[0]="..";
//Open Dir to parse
    if ($dh = opendir($dir))
    {
        //begin loop to read directory
        while (($filename = readdir($dh)) !== false){
            //discard . and .. directory pointers
            if (($filename != ".") && ($filename !=
"..")) 
            {
```

```
            $num_files++;
            $file_list[$num_files]=$filename;
            }//if . and ..
        }//while
    }
    closedir($dh);

[/dir]
```

It basically cycles through a dir, adding files to an array, and keeping a variable with the amount of files added.

If you have a newer version of PHP, then you can achieve the same as above in very few lines using the glob() function:
http://www.php.net/manual/en/function.glob.php
The use array_rand() to pick a random element:
http://www.php.net/manual/en/function.array-rand.php

CODE:
```
$theImages =  glob("*.jpg");
$image = $theImage[array_rand($theImages)];
```

Question 85: Word Automation with PHP

Is it possible to create a word doc of labels from a mysql database within the PHP site?

A: As long as PHP and Word are running on the same machine, it is possible using PHP's COM functions (http://www.php.net/manual/en/ref.com.php). You can't do it in a web-server environment.

There might be other ways to accomplish what you're trying to do, depending on what you intend to do with the data.

Question 86: Limit of Session Variables

All my session variables contain 3 digit numbers (1-999). Is there a limit on the number of active (i.e. holding data) session variables one can have at any time?

A: Since session stores are serialized and written to files on the server's hard drive between uses, the only practical limit is the size of the serial file imposed by your server's filesystem or the amount of memory available to the server.

In my own scripts, I have use session variables for shopping carts that did, in testing, hold hundreds of items with 4 or 5 pieces of information on each.

Question 87: fopen and fgets

I'm doing a login page. I've written the user information to a text file and see that it's delimited with a semi-colon. I can't seem to work around it, so I created a new variable that is made up of the user name and password with the semi-colon in between. When I echo the new variable, it appears to be the same as the line in the file. When I compare it in the if statement, it comes up as no match. Here is the code:

```php
<?php
$UserInfo=$_POST["UserName"];
$PasswordInfo=$_POST["Password"];
$VarToTest="$UserInfo:$PasswordInfo";

$fp = fopen ("users.txt", "r");
$check=0;
while (!feof ($fp) && ($check == 0))
{
    $content = fgets( $fp, 4096 );

    if ($content == $VarToTest)
    {
    $check = 1;
    }
    else
    {
    $check = 0;
    }
}

if ($check ==1)
    {
    echo "Welcome $UserName\n";
    echo "<a href='shop.html'>go shopping</a>";
    }
    else
    {
    echo "sorry, your information does not match our
records\n";
    echo "<a href='login.html'>try again</a>";
    }

fclose ($fp);
?>
```

What is wrong with my expression?

A: Try this code:

```
If ($VarToTest == trim($content)) $check = 1;
```

When you read a line from a file, it comes in with the terminating "\n". The trim() function will remove that character.

Also, since you've already initialized $check to 0, you don't need the else clause.

I would actually initialize the variable to FALSE, so the whole sequence would be:

```
CODE:
$check = FALSE;
while (($content = fgets($fp, 4096)) != FALSE)
{
    if ($content == $VarToTest) {
        $check = TRUE;
        continue; }
}
fclose ($fp);

if ($check)
    echo 'Welcome ' . $UserName. "<br>\n" . '<a
href="shop.html">go shopping</a>';
else
    echo 'Sorry, your information does not match our
records<br>'."\n".'<a href="login.html">Please try
again</a>';
```

As you can see, I shorted up the code a little. You don't need the braces "{ }" when the code block after an if statement is one line.

Storing unencrypted passwords in a text file is asking for trouble.

Question 88: Logical Operator problem

I can verify the IDNumber but now when I'm trying to also validate the password the user enters. I get this syntax error: Parse error: syntax error, unexpected T_IF in C:\www\htdocs\try.php on line 82

```php
CODE:
<?PHP
 if (isset($_POST['IDnumber'])) {
 $IDFound = "This is a valid Number";
 $IDNotFound = "This is not a valid Number";
 $Password = "TestPwd"
 If ($totalRows_Recordset2==1 AND
$_POST['Password']==$Password)
    {echo $IDFound;}
 Else
    {echo $IDNotFound;}
 }
 ?>
```

What is causing the error?

A: When PHP gives you a "parse error on line x", that means that line x in your script is the line where PHP realized it was confused by your script. It is not necessarily the line where the error actually is.

In general, start at line x and work your way backward. Doing that on your code finds this line:

```php
$Password = "TestPwd"
```

This should read:

```php
$Password = "TestPwd";
```

Question 89: Passing values from PHP to HTML

The site entry page (index.htm) asks for username/password, the Submit then passes the values to a PHP page for validation against the server database. If a visitor has permission, they go into HTML pages which contain mailto.

After moving into HTML page with mailto, how do I get the data back I had obtained in the previous PHP page to include in the mailto email?

A: Since mailto is a simple html call to start email programs with printed information, you can output any php code to it in the same way you would output anything else in php. The bigger question is why are you using clumsy, awkward and very client dependent call mailto? If you have PHP's very own mail() (and also great custom classes like phpmailer) available, you can do the job quicker, easier and more reliable.

If the only reason you're still using .html extension is the fact you need it to design the page in FrontPage, I am afraid that is hardly a good excuse for doing it. What happens if you open a page with .php extension (but no php code) in FrontPage?

Incidentally, there is an article about using php within frontpage on MS website: http://office.microsoft.com/en-us/assistance/HA011092991033.aspx

If nothing works, simply make a solid design with placeholders for code in FrontPage and then manually change them as you convert the static html page to dynamic php.

Question 90: Convert a UTC time to display quickly

I've got a UTC time from an LDAP query to active directory in the form of:

"YYYYMMDDHHMMSS.oZ"

Is there a quick function similar to the "date" function that will convert it to a more printable format?

A: PHP provides the function strtotime() to convert date strings to timestamp integers. The date() can then accept that integer as its optional second parameter.

However, strtotime() doesn't understand the format of "YYYYMMDDHHMMSS.oZ".

Through judicious insertion of dashes, spaces and colons, the string can be converted into something strtotime() understands: "YYYY-MM-DD HH:MM:SS"

One way to add the dashes is through a regular expression. There are certainly others:

CODE:
```php
<?php
$string = '20050609042311.0Z';

$string1 = preg_replace
('/^(\d{4})(\d{2})(\d{2})(\d{2})(\d{2})(\d{2})(.*)/',
'$1-$2-$3 $4:$5:$6', $string);

print date ('Y-m-d', strtotime($string1));

?>
```

Question 91: Get and print current file location in PHP

I want to print and place in an anchor (link) the name of the current file a user is viewing using php and html.

Using "ThisFile.html" as an example, I want to be able to print on the page:
'You are currently browsing -- <a href=[php code here?]>Whatever</a>'

I am using $_server('php_self') which works if the file ends with ".php". However, I want to be able to do this using just plain HTML pages. Is this possible?

A: PHP will just work with files that are interpreted by the server. If .html is not evaluating the PHP code, then you are out of luck since it is plain, static HTML.
You could revert to client side code using JavaScript and use document.location to populate the link.

Question 92: Best editor to print PHP code

I'm looking for an editor that allows me to print (color coded) my php code in customize font size. Right now, I can print in color but the code is always in that ugly courier font (too large a size) which wraps and makes it super hard to read.

What is the best editor to print a PHP code?

A: A pspad seems to do what you are asking for, it's freeware too.

If you are using windows, just associate the php extension with pspad, highlight the files you want to print, right-click and print!

Question 93: Displaying grouped report

I would like to create a report in the form of:

{RepName}
Mobile Number   Warranty   Label
...
...
...
...

[RepName]
Mobile Number   Warranty   Label
...
...
...

I would like to iterate through my query result set and each time there is a change in the Rep's name to first print out the name of the rep and then display a new table and then continue filling in the rows from that point.

Is there any construct within PHP that would allow me to accomplish this?

A: This is a basic programming technique which has mainly to do with 'remembering' the current rep.

Here are the basic steps:

1. Initialize a $currentRep variable with an empty string.
2. Iterate the result set in a while loop, e.g.
   while ($row = mysql_fetch_assoc($result)){ etc. }
3. Check first in the loop if the rep's name in the current row is the same or not.
4. If not the same, distinguish between an empty name (which is the initial run) or something in $currentRep. If there's something in the name you need to close the previous table with the appropriate tags - if empty that's not necessary as no table is open.
5. If not the same, open up a new table and set $currentRep to the new value.
6. Add table rows as you go.
7. After the final row the last table needs to be closed outside the while loop.

Question 94: Editing a text file

I have to administer a text file based comment system on my site:

```
$file = "./shouts.txt";
$fp = fopen($file, "r+");

rewind($fp);
fwrite($fp,$shout);
fclose($fp);
```

The shouts.txt file exists and is editable, i.e. has the right CHMOD values. Is there any way I can delete the entire contents of the file first, and then have it write in $shout?

A: Change the second parameter of fopen to "w".

```
So it should be:
$fp = fopen($file,"w");
```

Here is a link for other options in case you need them:

http://us2.php.net/manual/en/function.fopen.php

Question 95: Retrieve information from URL string

I am trying to check if a variable exists in the URL and if it does, make a decision on that for what to show.

Currently I have this setup:

CODE:
```
if(is_null($_GET['u']))
{
//Do this
}
else
{
//Do this
}
```

When the page appears and 'u' variable is not present, I get an indexing error. I do not want to use a form or post method. I would like to be able to just place it in a hyperlink and test for it. What method can I use?

A: You can use the following:

CODE:
```
if (isset($_GET['x']))
to check for existence.
```

Question 96: Emailing html file

I am trying to send an email after a user has registered an account online. I was wondering instead of retyping where I have to keep on concatenating a string of html code...

```
<?
$message ="<html>"
$message =."<title>google homepage</title>"
$message =."<head>blah blah blah</head>"
$message =.".... etc

?>
```

Is there a way where I could just email the file or copy and paste the code without editing it to be sent in the message variable?

A: The message must be read into memory. That's the only way to pass the message body to the mail() function.

If you don't like all the multiple concatenation lines, use one line. This will work:

$message = '<html><title>google homepsge</title></head>....';

This will work, too:

```
$message = '<hml>
<title>google homepage</title>
<head>blah blah blah</head>
.... etc';
```

If the message is static and you don't want to look at the message body in your script at all, you could put the message text into a file and use file_get_contents() to read the file into a variable.

Question 97: PHP and Operating System Detection

I have a custom popup script that works fine with Windows XP Professional but not with XP Home. I want to add a php detection script that will tell whether the user is using XP Home or XP Professional and then redirect the user according to these variables. What do I need to do this?

A: PHP runs on the server and it would detect the OS that is running on the server rather than that of the client. You will need to use JavaScript to detect client machine & settings.

Question 98: One PHP code for all seasons

Click on the leftnav for whichever month's news you want on the website. The PHP coding for each of the 12 pages is almost identical.

The only change is the heading - 'Our news for January' or 'Our news for April' and of course the name of the table, JanNews, FebNews, MarchNews, etc.

Is there a way for just the one page to handle the news for all of the year, for all of each of those 12 months?

So whichever month is chosen, I want the code to automatically change the code in those two or three places for whichever month's news is selected. Is there a code for this?

A: Of course there is, that's the beauty of PHP. Why write 12 scripts when one can do it all?

Here's a quick & dirty script...

CODE:
```
<?
for ($i=1;$i<13;$i++){
    $mnt = date('F',strtotime($i.'/1/2005'));
    $month_array[$mnt] = $mnt . 'News'; }

?>
<html>
<head></head>
<body>
<div class=lhcol>
<?
// set up left hand nav area
foreach ($month_array as $k=>$v) {
    echo '<a href=" . $_SERVER['PHP_SELF'] .
'?mnt='.$k.'">News for '.$k.'>'."<br>\n"; }
?>
</div>
<div class=mainarea>
<?
```

```php
if (isset($_GET['mnt'])) {
    echo '<h1>News for '. $_GET['mnt'] . "</h1>\n";
    $q = 'select * from '.
$month_array[$_GET['mnt']];
    $rs = @mysql_query($q);
    while ($rw = mysql_fetch_assoc($rs)) {
// I assumed your new was stored in a MySQL db
    }
}
?>
</body>
</html>
```

This is a very simple code sample. No error checking (or not much). Expand as necessary.

Question 99: Returning option variable

A form I'm working on requires an option box which concatenates variables from a 2 dimensional array into the select area. When a user selects from the list, I need to hold onto only the second part of the concatenation (Vopt[x][2]). In my example below, I'm trying to trap the value in Topt. If you paste the code below as 'option.php', maybe you can tell me what is wrong?

CODE:
```
<html>
<head>
<title>Option Menu</title>
</head>
<body>
<?php
$Vopt[0][1]="I" ;
$Vopt[0][2]="0,2" ;
$Vopt[1][1]="You" ;
$Vopt[1][2]="1,2" ;
$Vopt[2][1]="He/She/It" ;
$Vopt[2][2]="2,2" ;
$Vopt[3][1]="We" ;
$Vopt[3][2]="3,2" ;
$Vopt[4][1]="All You all" ;
$Vopt[4][2]="4,2" ;
$Vopt[5][1]="They" ;
$Vopt[5][2]="5,2" ;
Echo "<br> OPT: ".$_POST[opt]."<br>\n" ;
Echo "<br> TOPT: ".$_POST[topt]."<br>\n" ;
?>
<form action="option.php" method="POST">
<Select Name="opt">
<?php
for ($i = 0; $i <6; $i++)
{
if ( $_POST[opt] == $Vopt[$i][1]." - ".$Vopt[$i][2] )
    {
    echo "<option selected>", $Vopt[$i][1]." -
".$Vopt[$i][2], "</option>\n";
    echo "<input type='hidden' name='topt'
value=".'"'.$Vopt[$i][2].'"'.">\n";
    }
else
    {
```

```
    echo "<option>", $Vopt[$i][1]." - ".$Vopt[$i][2],
"</option>\n";
    echo "<input type='hidden' name='opt'
value=".'"'.$Vopt[$i][2].'"'.">\n";
    }
}
?>
</select>
<INPUT TYPE=SUBMIT NAME=SUBMIT VALUE="Display">
</FORM>
</body>
</html>
```

Is there an easy solution for this?

A: The solution is quite simple:
The <option> tag has a value attribute which defaults to the contained text if not set. All you need to do is print the desired values inside the value attribute.

CODE:
```
echo '<option value="'.$Vopt[$i][2].'">',
$Vopt[$i][1]." - ".$Vopt[$i][2], "</option>\n";
```

Question 100: Text orientation in PDF

Does anybody know how to print vertically oriented text using the PDFlib library of PHP?

A: The manual says:

Quote:

4.8.3 Aligning Text

Simple alignment: Our next goal is to rotate text such that its original lower left corner will be placed at a given reference point (see Figure 4.9). This may be useful, for example, for placing a rotated column heading in a table header: PDF_fit_textline(p, text, 5, 5, "orientate west");

This code fragment orientates the text to the west (90? counterclockwise) and then translates it the lower left corner of the rotated text to the reference point (5, 5).

Aligning text at a vertical line: Positioning text along a vertical line (i.e., a box with zero width) is a somewhat extreme case which may be useful nevertheless (see Figure4.10): PDF_fit_textline(p, text, 0, 0, "boxsize {0 600} position {0 50} orientate west"); This code fragment rotates the text, and places it at the center of the line from (0, 0) to (0, 600).

Acknowledgement

All the foregoing was culled from the following websites:

http://www.vbforums.com/forumdisplay.php?s=&daysprune=3
0&f=27

http://www.tek-tips.com/

http://www.zend.com/forums/index.php?t=index&S=07b74ba8
4e846d0bd76c61ae6cb73267

http://www.webmaster-talk.com/php-forum/

Index